2 BOOKS IN 1

A Radical Guide and Essential Strategies for Raising an Explosive Child and Learning Emotional Control Strategies with Organizing Solutions for Self-Regulate to Help Adult Women with ADHD

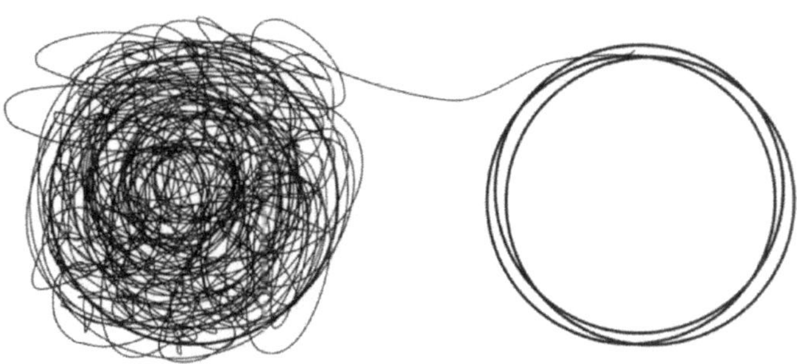

MARY JANE GOALS

Disclaimer

This publication is designed to provide competent and reliable information regarding the subject matter covered. However, it is sold with the understanding that the author

is not engaged in rendering professional or Nutrition advice. Laws and practices often vary from state and country to country and if medical or other expert assistance is required, the services of a professional should be sought. The author specifically disclaims any liability that is

incurred from use or application of the content of this book.

CONTENTS

BOOK 1:

ADHD RAISING AN EXPLOSIVE CHILD

The Complete Guide to Managing Your Emotions and Raising a Confident Child. Learn How to Recognize and Cope with Attention Deficit Disorder

BOOK 2:

WOMEN WITH ADHD

How to Overcome the Hidden Struggles of Living with ADHD. Embrace Neurodiversity and Learn the Best Emotional Control Strategies Thanks to the Power of Self-Discipline

ADHD

RAISING AN EXPLOSIVE CHILD

The Complete Guide To Managing Your Emotions And Raising A Confident Child. Learn How To Recognize And Cope With Attention Deficit Disorder.

MARY JANE GOALS

ADHD

Raising an Explosive Child

The Complete Guide to Managing
Your Emotions and Raising a Confident Child.
Learn How to Recognize and
Cope with Attention Deficit Disorder

MARY JANE GOALS

Introduction

Attention deficit hyperactivity disorder, known as ADHD, is currently one of the most common neurodevelopmental disorders affecting children and adolescents. These individuals are known to be active, impulsive, and have difficulty concentrating on certain tasks.

As the name suggests, these behaviors are typically closely correlated to one of the key symptoms of ADHD, cognitive issues.

Children with ADHD are not able to process information as easily as those without attention deficit hyperactivity disorder. However, the reason this happens is still unknown.

Researchers became interested in finding out why children with attention deficit hyperactivity disorder showed differences in their brains' chemistry compared to those without the disorder. These are referred to as chemical differences. To verify their theory, they administered traditional ADHD drugs to them, regulating their thinking and concentration.

After observation, the researchers concluded that children with attention deficit hyperactivity disorder had a more active dopamine transporter. That is a protein that regulates the level of dopamine in the user's brain.

If you have a child with ADHD, it is important that you first become aware of ADHD, what its possible causes are, and what you can do to help your child deal with the disorder's symptoms. Attention, deficit hyperactivity disorder, can cause many difficulties in children and adolescents, but there are many things you can do to help.

First, learn about the disorder, be informed, and understand what your child is dealing with in this situation. Do not be afraid to talk and ask your child's doctor or school about any concerns you may have.

Second, do not let your feelings, emotions, or reactions hinder the process of healing. Managing your response to your child with

ADHD is very important. If you give in to the frustration you face, you are only harming your child and yourself.

Third, you can help your child get the medical diagnosis he/she needs to start the healing process. That is important as it is required to access the appropriate treatment, including medication. Family doctors or pediatricians can begin the long process of diagnosis.

Fourth, do what you can as a parent. When you spend time with your child, actively engage yourself in the activity. That means, if they are watching television, you watch with them, not just in the room. Listening to music? Put in an earphone and participate. Even cook food together.

Finally, do not be afraid to seek the professional help of a counselor. Counselors are trained to help parents deal with the mental stress and burden of raising a child with ADHD. They can give you the skills to teach your child to curb the effects of ADHD and help you build a stronger relationship with your child.

A single and exact cause of ADHD has not fully been established nor understood. Still, it has been thought that the condition is caused by a combination of genetic and environmental factors. Environmental factors are those that come from your child's surroundings. These factors include diet, drugs, alcohol, tobacco, television, and limited time spent with parents.

Although there is an ongoing debate between psychologists and psychiatrists on the true cause of ADHD, it has been established that it is a biological disorder. It is classified as brain impairment, and even though there are genetic factors that come into play, there is no single established gene that causes ADHD. However, researchers believe it is most likely caused by multiple genes interacting together.

In children, those with classic ADHD are typically diagnosed after age five. If you or your spouse have ADHD, there is a chance that your children, both boys, and girls, will have a 50 percent chance of having this condition. ADHD can also be hereditary, meaning if one parent has it, their children are more likely to have the disorder.

On the other hand, the environmental factors listed above can also contribute to the development of ADHD, but only as very small factors. For example, research has shown that the less exposure a child has to cigarettes in their daily life, the less likely they will be diagnosed with the condition.

It is a rare genetic disorder that leads to a deficiency in neurotransmitters, which are chemicals in the brain that carry messages between cells.

It is no surprise that children with ADHD can develop behavioral and emotional problems from being constantly frustrated. Although there is no single known cause for ADHD, many factors are confirmed to be involved. These factors include genetics, diet, limited parental care, early childhood problems, brain injuries or infections, and family environment.

In ADHD children, the brain's action begins to take longer to respond and respond with muddy and unclear expectations. We know this as the brain "forgets" information a lot quicker than it should.

These children are more likely to be hyperactive, easily distracted, impulsive, inattentive, bored, chronically active, and cannot focus. They tend to be restless, will not sit still for long, and speak very quickly and in noisy voices. Many have learning difficulties and are usually impulsive, can soon lose things, and are poorly coordinated, with poor handwriting. Many often tantrum or hit or bite other people and often create difficulties for themselves and their families.

Some children will have many of these symptoms and impairment in many areas of social and school life. These children have a high risk of dropping out of school later in life and have a low employment rate.

The diagnosis of ADHD is not easy. Other conditions have similar symptoms, but they are not as severe. We know that ADHD is a neuro-behavioral disorder, and some signs are far more than just normal behavior. These children will often have extreme and odd behavior and impairments in social and school life. The symptoms will be learned behavior and the way the mind has been wired through the years.

What Is ADHD and What Does it Mean?

What does it mean to have ADHD?

ADHD is a term coined to describe children who have an attention deficit disorder. It is best understood as an extreme form of what has become known as hyperactivity disorder or AHD, and it generally affects the brain's ability to focus on tasks and produce a coordinated, calm, and mindful way of interacting with the world around you.

A disorder of this sort doesn't typically pose any significant physical, behavioral, or psychological symptoms, aside from having difficulty sustaining focused attention. It's not a mental illness; it's a neurological condition that leaves people without an organized mental strategy for managing their behavior.

According to experts, ADHD is so strongly correlated with antisocial behavior in children that it's often thought of as the marker for a bad early childhood: one that led to what is referred to as the "tyranny of the intrusive thoughts," which will have a big impact on children's ability to successfully manage their lives and their emotions as they mature.

ADHD is a condition that encompasses a collection of symptoms associated with impulsive or hyperactive behavior that can make it very difficult to manage your impulses and focus on the tasks that matter to you. Symptoms include restlessness, impulsivity, hyperactivity, and distraction. They can disrupt a child's daily life, but they can also affect how a child communicates with others and how well he or she interacts with the world around them.

Despite being a useful term in describing children, ADHD is an oversimplified description of an extremely complicated set of problems. It's not an illness that's explained by an anatomical or metabolic malfunction, or by a chemical imbalance. Instead, it's a developmental disorder that makes people's brains behave more immaturely than they would normally, even though it affects those who have the condition differently.

The term "ADHD" is often mistakenly used to refer only to the most extreme form of hyperactivity in children, but ADHD refers to a specific pattern of symptoms that can affect the way a person processes information, and the way that person deals with everyday tasks. These symptoms can range from abnormal sleeping patterns, difficulty organizing or sustaining attention, and rapid speech and reaction times to uncontrolled physical or verbal behaviors, such as repetitive movements or restlessness.

There are a few symptoms that are specifically linked with hyperactivity disorder: symptoms of distraction and drowsiness, as well as being restless or fidgety, making it hard to sit still, and displaying an increased need for stimulation. It's this last characteristic that many parents and educators attribute to ADHD and assume it causes children's behavior problems.

However, ADHD can impact children of all ages, from infants and toddlers to adolescents and adults, and most commonly manifests in kids between the ages of 5 and 17. Despite this fact, ADHD is usually thought of as an issue of children only, leading them to perform poorly in school, engage in risky behavior, and suffer from some social and emotional problems.

How Can ADHD Be Used for Anger Management?

Many doctors and therapists see ADHD and anger as at least somewhat related. That's because, according to the American Psychiatric Association, anger is often considered to be an antecedent to ADHD.

Both conditions are characterized by "inattention, hyperactivity, impulsivity, and/or distractibility," the APA says. As a result, a person who has ADHD is more likely to experience "irritability, anxiety, irritability, hostility, and impulsiveness that may increase or decrease" with "stress," the group says.

If you suspect your ADHD-suffering friend or a family member has anger problems, then you should watch out for certain behavioral symptoms, like:

- Overly harsh or unforgiving speech.

- Controlling and coercive behaviors.

- The inability to have and maintain satisfying relationships.

Uncontrollable outbursts, even when there's no real provocation.

Jumping to conclusions and making unwise or thoughtless decisions.

In the short term, the best place for someone with anger issues to seek help is with a mental health professional that can provide long-term, or even long-term, strategies for managing the condition.

In the long-term, some therapists say that taking antidepressants, or even using ADHD medication as a self-treat, can be helpful, as they can help manage emotions and behaviors. (Most antidepressants used to treat ADHD are also available as a long-term treatment.),

As a last resort, if a person is unable to get into a mental health professional's office or is unable to find a suitable one in their area, they may reach out to a suicide crisis line. Crisis hotline counselors often work closely with mental health professionals and, if a person is suicidal, they can help them find appropriate resources in their areas, such as a local crisis center, a doctor, or even a support group.

Finally, ADHD sufferers who are ready to seek help can turn to therapy — or try an online therapy course — to learn how to manage their anger and teach them better coping skills.

Types of ADHD

(A) Hyperactive-Impulsive ADHD

People with this type of ADHD appear to be constantly moving or doing something, as the name implies. Children with this condition are frequently seen running around and touching various things, playing with various objects, or talking about various topics at a rapid pace. They will have difficulty staying still, have the tendency to fidget or move around in their seats, or will display certain tics (tapping their fingers on the table, tapping their pens, moving their toes and fingers, etc.).

For teens or adults, this type of ADHD most often manifests in internal restlessness and doing too many things simultaneously. These individuals feel the overwhelming need to keep busy and to multitask. The impulsiveness will show when these individuals lose control over immediate reactions, despite the possible consequences. It isn't uncommon for these individuals to blurt out what they are thinking regardless of appropriateness, to express unbridled emotion, and rash behavior in general. Waiting can be extremely difficult, even during mundane tasks like waiting for their turn during games.

A person must exhibit 5 or more of the following symptoms for at least 6 months in order to be diagnosed with this type of ADHD, as well as a significant negative impact on the person's overall functioning:

- Fidgeting, unnecessary movements of the hands or feet, squirming, etc.
- The inability to sit still or the sudden departure during situations where they are required to stay in one place (e.g. abrupt leaving of the classroom, leaving the workplace, etc.)
- Blurting out thoughts or words inappropriately, answering without fully hearing questions, etc.
- Excessive talking
- Tendency to interrupt others or intrude on others; seemingly uncontrollable
- Difficulties when waiting for turns, waiting in line, waiting for packages, etc.
- Overwhelming sense of restlessness, as if being "driven by a motor"

(B) Inattentive Type of ADHD

An individual with inattentive ADHD will have difficulty focusing and sticking with one activity or idea. They frequently drop things in the middle of a process and may become easily bored with the task at hand. However, they may be able to finish a project successfully given that it is something they are genuinely interested in. It is important to note that consciously allotting time and energy on a particular activity that is new and difficult will be especially stressful for people with this type of ADHD. These individuals will often find it difficult to take homework, whether at school or at their job. Their finished products may also be of poor quality, due to mistakes borne out of frustration or cramming until the very last minute.

The interesting difference is that people with inattentive ADHD often display minimal hyperactivity, but a significant problem in terms of focus, concentration, and attentiveness. These people may appear to be slow or spaced out, easily disoriented, or lethargic. They may also have difficulty understanding verbal or written instructions, and errors in their work are common. Though it may seem that they are quietly working on the task at hand, they may not be fully paying attention to what they are doing.

Socially, however, these individuals fare better than those with other forms of the condition. To be diagnosed with this form of ADHD, the individual must experience 5 or more of the following symptoms, coupled with a significant negative impact on the person's general well-being.

- Carelessness with regards to work and output; often observed to make careless mistakes in school, in the workplace, and with other tasks
- Significant difficulties in focusing or sustaining attentiveness while performing tasks or activities
- Problems in actively listening to others
- Difficulties in organizing different aspects of their lives; often observed to miss deadlines, producing messy work, having messy surroundings, etc.
- Easily distracted by unimportant physical or mental stimuli
- Difficulties keeping track of their belongings or keeping track of what they need to do

- A lack of interest in things that require mental rigor
- Significant forgetfulness in daily activities such as chores, errands, paying bills, appointments, etc.

<u>(C) Combined Type of ADHD</u>

As implied by the name, a person with combined ADHD exhibit symptoms from both the hyperactive-impulsive type and the inattentive type of ADHD for an extended period coupled with negative effects on their general wellbeing.

ADHD Types of Symptoms and Characteristics of a Child with ADHD

If you're like many out there, you might think that ADHD is over-diagnosed, and that everyone has the 8 symptoms. While it can be easy to dismiss a diagnosis as "just not for me," it's possible to have only one or two of these 8 symptoms.

Let's go through each symptom individually so you can see what they mean and how they look in real-life!

1) ADD/ADHD: Inattention

Inattention can be described as an inability to focus on tasks, jobs, or activities - even if they are things we enjoy doing. It's likely that some tasks are completed at a more successful rate than others. Inattention can have various levels and severities, so it's not always easy to see in the everyday person.

If your child is diagnosed with ADHD, you are likely to notice that even when they are participating in an activity they enjoy, their mind tends to wander. For example: playing a video game or watching a movie. They may suddenly begin talking about something else completely unrelated to the game or movie, which may seem out of character for the child. It's not uncommon for children with ADHD to answer their own questions before anyone has a chance to respond - they simply don't have the ability to keep their thoughts focused on a singular topic during those times... or at any time.

2) ADD/ADHD: Lack of Focus

Inability to focus can be nearly impossible to see in oneself because we are accustomed to dealing with this on a day-to-day basis. When our minds wander, we move on to another thought or activity without ever realizing it.

This symptom may even cause your child or partner to express what seems like boredom in the moment - it's not that they're bored, but rather that their mind is somewhere else and has simply wandered off course from the original conversation topic, situation, plot of the movie, etc.

3) ADD/ADHD: Poor Time Management

Poor time management is often linked to a lack of focus. Someone with ADHD may feel out of sorts in a classroom because they are unable to focus on the lesson or discussion, and instead will constantly be doodling on their paper or daydreaming. Another example is when you ask your child or partner to pick up groceries before returning home in an hour and they don't return for two hours, without groceries... and with no recollection of what happened during that time period.

4) ADD/ADHD: Poor Impulse Control

Impulsivity is one of the most obvious and common symptoms of ADHD. Someone diagnosed with ADHD may struggle with the ability to control themselves during everyday situations. This can be hard to notice when you're around someone who is able to adapt well in a variety of circumstances, but when you're just trying to use a payphone or waiting quietly in line at the grocery store... many won't have a clue!

5) ADD/ADHD: Exaggerated Emotions

When your child is "emotionally out of control" it's not something that they are aware of - it's something that happens automatically. For example, a child may be happy to see their grandmother when she comes for a visit, and then an hour later they're sobbing, seemingly without reason. It may have been that they were playing happily with a favorite toy previously in the day and then, suddenly, something happened that reminded them of their lost pet goldfish.

Whether it's a good or bad memory from the past affects the severity of emotions as well - a death in the family might even cause someone with ADHD to become inconsolable. The best way to show your understanding is by simply listening while allowing your loved one to express how they are feeling at any given moment.

6) ADD/ADHD: Hyper focus

When someone with ADHD is hyper focused, they might have a difficult time breaking off of an activity. Often when we are deeply involved in a hobby or other experience it's very easy to forget that others exist. For example, when someone with ADHD sits down to play a video game and is so focused on the game that they lose track of time - hours may go by before they realize it's time for dinner!

It's not unusual for someone with ADHD to play games for long periods, even on the same day, without any problems. They may have trouble relating to other people because they are so consumed by one thing at a time. However, when they're not hyper focused in this manner they are likely to be very outgoing and social.

7) ADHD/ADD: Sensory Sensitivity

Sensory sensitivity is one of the most misunderstood symptoms of ADHD, and it can be quite intimidating for those who aren't quite certain what is going on or why. Someone with sensory sensitivity may have trouble wearing certain fabrics or even soft materials against bare skin. They may even have sensitivities to sounds which may manifest themselves as being overly loud or amplified - a ticking clock or a dog's barking are examples of this in everyday life.

Sensory sensitivities can play a role in food preferences as well some may be repulsed by the smell of certain foods or be unable to digest certain kinds of foods. It's not uncommon for someone with ADHD to eat one food at breakfast, another at lunch and yet still another at dinner! This doesn't mean that they are engaging in an avoidance behavior - it simply means that they are sensitive to tastes and textures which are uncomfortable to them.

8) ADHD/ADD: Poor Motor Skills

Poor motor skills can have a big impact on any child or adult with ADHD, because it might make it incredibly difficult for them to participate in organized sports. Instead of being able to play a game that involves coordination and teamwork, they might be left on the sidelines because they can't catch the ball or swing the bat!

This doesn't mean that your child is not athletic - instead it may simply mean that he plays best when a game is adapted to fit his unique capabilities. For example, if he's being encouraged by parents or teammates to do something, he's not completely comfortable with... this might only lead to failure and disappointment.

Parent's Guide to Dealing with Attention Deficit Hyperactivity Disorder

The effects on parents of raising a child with ADHD are profound. For one, parenting is a lot harder than it usually is. Children with ADHD seem to have difficulty completing tasks and following directions, so when you as the parent are telling them something they often just don't listen to you because their minds elsewhere. Having a child with ADHD demands precious time, money, and patience from parents.

Children with ADHD can be very frustrating for their parents. Arguments between the two types of children may also arise because they constantly want things that will result in long-term rewards while those without ADHD will only do things for immediate gratification.

Children with ADHD also pose a risk to their parents. This can lead to physical fights that put the parent in danger from other kids, as well as the child with ADHD who often resorts to assault in attempts to protect themselves or their parents.

Due to the attention deficit disorder, children with ADHD may have a hard time keeping up with schoolwork and their grades may suffer (often even if they are above average students). Studies have also shown that children with ADHD have a harder time reading social cues, making their social interactions more problematic. This can make it hard for the child to get along with other students, his or her life at school may be affected by this and sometimes even split from the family because of the added stress and constant fighting.

As time goes on, ADHD symptoms can cause havoc in a child's personal and academic life.

ADHD has been proven to decrease a child's ratings in their academic success, emotional development, and self-esteem. It is also shown to cause a decrease in social abilities due to the inability to recognize social cues.

A study conducted at the University of Toronto, Canada indicated that there was no relationship between the severity of ADHD symptoms and treatment outcome for adults who had been diagnosed with ADHD when they were children. The study was performed using a database of over 37,000 children under the age of 15 who had been treated for ADHD since 1972. The researchers found that there was "no significant association between ADHD severity and adult functioning or treatment outcome."

Because symptoms can vary widely from child to child, it is difficult to predict long-term effects of ADHD on any given child. However, some persistent problems have been found in different studies with longitudinal follow-up. These studies include the following:

Researchers found that those who experienced their first episode of hyperactive behavior before age 7 had higher rates of symptoms persisting in late childhood and adolescence than those who did not have overt hyperactivity at age 7. According to the authors' conclusions, this could be due to the relatively long interval between onset and treatment or could be an indicator of a less favorable outcome in individuals with early-onset ADHD.

Intelligence has not been found to differ meaningfully between children with ADHD and those without. This is also true for IQ levels later in life. However, studies have found that inattention is negatively correlated with academic achievement, even when controlling for IQ. In addition, some studies have found that hyperactivity can negatively affect academic performance but not intelligence.

Children who have been treated for ADHD are at a higher risk of substance abuse throughout their lives. These addictions can be caused by the lack of focus that was originally intended to be treated by the medication in the first place. As time goes on, children with untreated or unrecognized ADHD are more likely to develop addiction and substance abuse problems than those whose treatment was successful.

ADHD can affect an individual's ability to form and maintain intimate relationships. Studies have shown that children with ADHD are more likely to form intimate relationships in which one of the partners is not their spouse, as well as less likely to be married. When a child does become married, they are more likely to report arguments and conflict within their marriage and less likely to be committed to their spouse than those who are not diagnosed with ADHD. Children with ADHD are also more likely to express dissatisfaction in their relationships than those without, as well as experiencing more marital problems in general.

Children diagnosed with ADHD show a pattern of rejection by friends when they reach adolescence. However, although these friendships are more likely to end in the early teens, they tend to be stable later on.

Anxiety disorders can worsen during times of stress or in the presence of a stressor, and they may develop alongside the symptoms of ADHD. The most common anxiety disorders among adults with ADHD are generalized anxiety disorder and panic disorder. Depression can also affect those who have been diagnosed with ADHD as well as those who have never been diagnosed with it.

However, they are less likely to abuse drugs and alcohol or be treated for addiction than those without ADHD. They are less likely to be dependent on others or put other individuals in a position of power over themselves, instead preferring independence.

The cognitive deficits and executive functions associated with ADHD can cause problems in an academic setting, leading to low achievement among individuals with ADHD compared with the general population, even when they have similar IQ scores. When they do achieve good grades, it is often due to hard work and strategies such as studying more than their peers.

How to Raise ADHD Children?

One of the most common complaints about ADHD and hyperactivity among children is that they are too difficult to raise. However, those who have had experience with these issues know that it can be done, but it requires patience and persistence. When you have kids who are hyperactive, you may need to learn how to help them as well as discipline them in order for you both to live productive lives.

It was once believed that hyperactivity and inattention were a result of poor mental and physical health. The problem that has been identified as most prevalent in today's children is ADHD. The disorder is also referred to as attention-deficit hyperactivity disorder (ADHD). In many cases, these disorders can be traced back to traumatic experiences that the child may have dealt with as a child or even prior to birth.

According to research, the most common form of behaviorally based ADHD is the predominantly inattentive type. This type ranges from mild to moderate in severity. What this means for your child is that they may have difficulties with attention and concentration. Often, insomniacs are thought to be so because of their inability to concentrate on a task for any length of time. When you have a child who has inattentive ADHD, you should expect to have to deal with problems such as:

- Problems with memory.
- Problems with organizational skills.
- Poor attention span, which makes it difficult to pay attention or complete tasks.
- Problems carrying out instructions and following through on commitments.

Looking on the Bright Side of Being the Parent of an ADHD Child the Energy: Lots of Energy!

While every bit of this information is useful because knowledge is power, there is one thing we have yet to discuss—the bright side of ADHD. You are probably reading this and thinking about all the negative behavioral and emotional issues. You are probably wondering how it is possible to be optimistic about a neurobiological disorder, especially one that is affecting the lives of your child and your family. But ADHD is not a prison sentence defined as life with no chance of parole. It is not a prison at all, especially when you change the way you view the disorder. Now, it is time to examine the good parts of ADHD.

The Positive Side/Good Side of ADHD

The first step in examining the positive side of ADHD is to transform your perspective. Stop looking at it from a negative viewpoint. Stop dwelling on the bad side of the behavioral issues and start looking at them as beneficial personality attributes. For each negative behavioral trait, there is an opposite—a "mirror" trait that ignores the negativity and focuses solely on the positive. As you can see, it is all about perspective and how you choose to view each behavior.

Impulsive behavior – Creative energy

Moody and irritable – Sensitive and compassionate

Easily distracted – Curious about the world around them

Restless and hyperactive – Energetic and ready for adventure

Stubborn – Determined.

Pushy and forward – Enthusiastic and assertive

When you focus on the "mirror" qualities of your child's behavior, you discover an entirely new way of living. Instead, you and your ADHD child can find new avenues to explore by using his "mirror" traits. There will still be times when those negative behaviors rear their ugly heads. But now you have the knowledge and skill set to deal with the negative behaviors swiftly, turning a potentially heated encounter into a positive situation.

In addition to finding the "mirror" qualities of your ADHD child, there are other positives to having ADHD. The ADHD mind might come across as unfocused and distractible, constantly leaping from one thought to another. However, this particular quality can come in quite handy for solving problems. As the mind of your ADHD child examines a problem with a peer, he is likely to sort through solutions faster than the non-ADHD child. While the non-ADHD child is still evaluating the first or second possible solution, your child has probably evaluated all of the solutions and may even be ready to solve the problem. ADHD children observe so many small details around them as they try to take in everything they see and hear. Your ADHD child is probably hearing much more than you realize. Just because your child appears to be involved in a different activity does not mean he is not also paying attention to your conversation. So, you may want to think twice before discussing adult matters in front of him.

Even though your ADHD child might have to work twice as hard as others, this is not necessarily a type of handicap. Instead, knowing that goals do not come as easily to him often intensifies the resolve of your ADHD child. His increased sense of determination pushes him to try and try again until he reaches his goal. Having this sort of determination may come across at times as stubbornness, but when you look at the "mirror" quality, you and your child will realize that persevering can be quite fulfilling. ADHD children are also not always unfocused. When they find an activity or task that excites them and keeps them intrigued, they can actually become intensely focused. This intense focus is so captivating that they often forget the entire world around them. Focusing like this can be quite helpful in completing projects, reading books, and overall learning.

Another positive side of ADHD is the seemingly endless amount of energy within your child. This type of infinite energy is useful in extracurricular activities, such as sports. Your ADHD child will probably want to participate in as many activities as possible.

Baseball, football, and track are good examples for burning off that energy supply. While you may be concerned with injuries or worried that your child might fail, his thoughts are somewhere else. He is not as likely to be afraid of failure because learning to live with ADHD has taught him to persevere and push forward, no matter what. Even taking a family hike in the hills will be an adventure for your ADHD child. Not only does your child expend some extra energy, but he also gets the chance to spend time with his family. All of this physical activity not only keeps boredom at bay, but it is also good for your child's physical health.

Another encouraging aspect of ADHD is your child's ability to be compassionate and accepting of others. What someone might see as overly emotional is just your child being deeply in tune with his emotions and being unable to hold them inside. Sure, this can be trying at times, but in times of crisis, such as when a loved one passes away, you can almost bet that your ADHD child will be a great source of comfort. Compassion comes easily to your ADHD child. He understands and connects with emotions. In fact, ADHD children are often described as having the biggest hearts and sensitive souls. It is not uncommon to find your child crying during emotional movies because of his enhanced sense of compassion.

Your ADHD child is also likely to have a very accepting personality. It will not matter if a potential friend seems "different" than everyone else. This is because your ADHD child is already special himself, so he understands what the other child is feeling. Your ADHD child does not care if a peer is the "underdog." A friend is a friend, and your child will enjoy having a new companion to play with and share creative energy. ADHD children have big personalities to match their big hearts. They make friends easily because they have such an interest in the world and what is happening around them. They have a zest for life that draws others' attention to them like moths to a flame.

One very important "mirror" trait is creativity. Your ADHD child is full of thoughts and ideas that need an outlet. His imagination is running wild at all hours of the day and night. Help your child to harness that creativity in a constructive way. Give your child a sketchbook or notebook so that he has a place to write down his thoughts and ideas, a place to draw the images that never seem to stop playing in his mind. You never know—maybe he will become the next big inventor! At the very least, the two of you can have interesting conversations about his thoughts and ideas. It is also a good idea if you embrace your ADHD child's imagination. Go ahead, get on the floor and play with your child. Maybe it is with Legos, maybe it is with a racetrack, and maybe it is just the two of you pretending to be characters in a fantasy land. Let your child's wild imagination help you release the kid inside.

ADHD can be difficult to deal with every day. There is no doubt that the constant struggle to modify and cope with behaviors is hard on your ADHD child, as well as the rest of the family. However, keeping things in perspective—especially a positive perspective— will help make each day just a little bit easier. This positive outlook will also rub off onto your ADHD child, encouraging him to embrace his differences and live his very best life for the rest of his life.

Living a Normal Life with ADHD

One of your primary concerns as a parent is probably how to maintain a normal life for your ADHD child, as well as for the rest of your family unit. All parents want well-behaved children that grow up to be contributing members of society. You may wonder if ADHD is going to hold your child back from reaching his full potential. Disruptive behaviors are also going to wear on your nerves, along with your family's nerves. There may be times when you find yourself wishing that your child could just be "normal." But your child is normal. He may not be like the average child, but he is normal. What you mean is that you wish your child did not have ADHD disrupting his life. You simply cannot dwell on the way things might have been—ADHD is a part of your lives now.

When talking about living a normal life with an ADHD child, you must think about the meaning of normal. One person's normal is another person's chaos. Just as you have to turn negative behaviors into positive "mirror" attributes, you need a positive outlook on life if you expect any sense of normalcy. Ask yourself what it means to you to have a normal life. Then, ask your ADHD child what it means to him. Compare your answers and you might just be surprised. A normal life for your family unit is not going to be like any other family. This is simply because values vary—what is important to one person may not be important to another. Just like that famous movie says, "Stupid is as stupid does." The same applies to normal. Your normal life may not look like everyone else's— but it is normal for you and your family—that is what really counts in the big picture. No one else is living your life for you, so no one else has the right to tell you what is and is not normal.

No longer will you throw your hands up in the air and wonder why he is behaving in such a manner. With an ADHD diagnosis, you now know why. You also have the skills to handle every situation, even the bad ones properly. Being professionally diagnosed with ADHD is your child's first step to a better and more normal life. From that point on, between treatment and therapy, your child's behaviors are only going to improve. It may not be easy, but once you and your ADHD child have discovered what works best for him, life will be much easier on both of you.

Managing ADHD Behavior Away from Home

Finally, you have to leave the house, so handling ADHD behavior in the outside world is crucial. It can be dangerous to travel. For fact, if your child goes outside limits and does damage to the property of others, the result may be costly. Even, if you do not curtail the ADHD actions of your child, you risk not fulfilling your errands and upsetting strangers. When she handled herself, it would be fine, so how can you get that to happen?

PROBLEMS IN THE CAR

The new relationship you build with your child will help immensely wherever you go, but during car rides, certain unusual issues that arise. It is both aggravating and risky to drive if your kid is misbehaving. You may be in a rush sometimes, and if your daughter doesn't want to help, she will ruin anything.

Solutions

You want your daughter to put on her seat belt without being told to do so, but if she's upset with something else, she may refuse. It makes better sense to look into the source of her annoyance than to focus only on her lack of compliance. Because the backseat can be lonely, by being proactive, you can also avoid negative attention. In a conversation, you can include your daughter, pack items of interest to her, or play a game with her to make the trip less lonely and boring.

When, when driving, your child starts a commotion, you may be worried about health. You may need to find a place for the car to rest and wait for it to settle down. Yeah, maybe you're late, but it's your best option. Let your child know, "Seeing more than one child ride with you is safe to drive only if we sit in our seats and get along." When you return to the lane, though, make sure the kids stop fighting and do something else, even if it just looks out the window. If they are not distracted from the conflict, the fighting can resume quickly.

WHO SITS WHERE?

When there is constant disagreement over the seating arrangement in the car, apply the same techniques that you would use to minimize conflict within the household; help the kids figure out the sharing system they want to use. Do this before your next trip: ask the kids if they have any suggestions to fix the problem at a time when everyone is calm. Every child may have a special seating choice, but as long as the kids find out what works for them, everything is going to be fine. Make sure that their program correctly informs them, or it is unlikely to be effective, who has first preference at specific times. You don't want to keep track of whose turn it's for the seat you want.

USING THE BATHROOM

Trips are often long, and access to a toilet is not always easy. Your daughter may insist that she doesn't have to go to the bathroom until you go, but she may start complaining that she has to use the toilet shortly after she leaves. You should pause to comply easily but try to find a solution which reduces the discomfort if the situation is routine. Let her know: "It's a long trip and finding a bathroom will be hard. Want to use the bathroom now to make you more relaxed while we're driving?" If she says no, you might add,' We'd be happy to wait for you,' as a way to make her rethink.

Help your child get into the bathroom routine before leaving. Model what you'd like her to do and ask if she'd like to take a turn. Start the journey whether or not she is going. There may be considerable difficulty if events play poorly but try to stay relaxed as she pays attention to her own pain. She will eventually learn that she's better off modeling your actions, and you're not going to have to say a thing about it.

PROBLEMS IN THE STORE

If you're looking for something she likes, your daughter may be very cooperative. But when she feels compelled to buy for others, her actions may be dramatically different. As is often the case, once she lacks the authority to determine what happens, the ADHD conduct of your daughter is sparked and intensified.

Solutions

If you're in good mood, your child will behave more, so you have significant influence. Talking about the favorite topics of discussion for your child can also help make unnecessary shopping less annoying. But most notably, if your child has more insight into what is going on, your child will probably comply more. If you're shopping for food, for example, you might ask her when she wants to help you decide what to get. Older kids might be happy to help you find bargains. Others may want to read the list of groceries or push the cart.

The bottom line is that when you and your child get along positively and share authority, ADHD behavior will be less frequent. Try to find the "sweet spot" where you get enough space for her to fit you easily so that you can complete the order. This is hard to achieve, but it can be achieved, and during shopping excursions, this has the biggest long-term effect on the rate of ADHD behavior.

RESOLVING PUBLIC MISBEHAVIOR

When you're out and about, things may not always go smoothly, so what do you do if your child acts up? If necessary, you should disregard or avoid the actions, but encouraging it to be loud and disruptive is not always acceptable to others. There may also be dangers when she's exuberant in public places that you don't want to play out.

Sadly, once your conduct is disrespectful or dangerous, you may have to physically stop your child or leave the store. In some situations, after a short time, it may be possible to re-enter the shop if your child settles down and you feel assured that when you return to the store, all will be optimistic.

Still, however, you might have to go back. It is crucial for your child to understand that her behaviors have a ripple effect in these circumstances. Such negative side effects can be illustrated. For starters, "Because we haven't done our shopping, we're going to have to go back later, and I'm not going to be able to make the dessert I was preparing of tonight." If the problem goes on, you might want to go one step farther. You might suggest that your daughter spend some of her own money to pay for the return trip, pointing out the positives of this option (e.g., this compensates others for having inconvenienced them, and it might mitigate their difficult feelings against her). When she offers reimbursement, everyone benefits.

Like when dealing with hygiene issues, you might also ask your child if she'd like to stay home next time and use some of her own money to pay someone to keep her company. She thus carries some

of the burden of refusing to satisfy the family agenda. Offer her choices, but also let her know that it may cost her some decisions.

PEER RELATIONSHIPS

Is your child accusing other kids for achieving a sense of superiority? Trying to "buy" friends by giving away personal items, displaying low self-esteem? Should she whine of mistreatment in order to get you to run her defense? Will she always sit on the playground by herself or just play with kids out of the common circle? If so, you might want to change it. You want a fun social life for your child and feel comfortable interacting with a variety of people.

Misbehaving with Peers

Quite often, her conduct becomes excessive when a child with ADHD meets another rambunctious child. If she behaves stupidly and doesn't try to meet standards, she stops feeling inferior, and when she plays with another cap tester, there is no loss. There is power in numbers, and when she teams up with a "bad friend," your daughter gathers influence and leverage.

Solutions

You can try to keep your child away from other kids who act out. This can, however, give your child the impression of being weak and easily manipulated. Another approach is to make her realize why she is mistaken and help her handle what happens when she faces negative influences successfully. This approach sends her the impression that in her setting, she will show herself and bring about change. She will see herself as a leader with good sense. You might say, "Your friend might be clever enough to imitate you when you're playing together."

You might also ask your daughter how she feels about getting in trouble and raise the question, "How do you want others to see you?" You can help her work out what to do when others push the envelope to find out if she's scared that if she doesn't join, others will make fun of her.

They may also question whether the cap checking is acceptable because the tricks may be misplaced ways of gaining attention or forms of weakening authority. Let your child know that addressing her problem behavior with her peers has a key advantage: taking them on family excursions makes it fun.

Doubting Acceptability

If your daughter doubts, she's reasonable to others, she will find it harder to act fairly. Perhaps when she clowns around, she encourages others to grin, but the unfortunate side effect is that she gets attention for immature behavior. She briefly takes advantage of habits that will inevitably not serve her well. If that's the case, you might say, "Do you believe you're going to have to show off or do something dumb to make people like you?" Then ask, "How is this going to work for you?" When she thinks it goes poorly, inquire, "I wonder if there are other ways to attract them?" You want to maintain your child's great sense of humor, but you don't want her to be crazy or dumb. She has many qualities that other people will admire, and you want her to bring out her best foot. Her actions with ADHD that diminish significantly when she is socially comfortable and confident that she is a friendly person. Additionally, her choice of friends will probably change if she feels good about herself.

Supporting Social Development

If your child is on the younger side, she'll probably repeat a lot of habits she experiences with other adults within the family. If she is demanding and possessive with you, with her playmates, she may also be demanding and possessive. When family members manipulate or disrespect her, or others give her a hard time, she can overreact or display fear. It is important to nurture habits that fit well with non-family members for these reasons. If you want her to communicate, accept social boundaries, and conduct with her peers assertively, improve her ability to connect within the group.

It is also helpful to give your child an opportunity to interact with other kids while encouraging their social development. So, she's going to increase her social skills. Encourage her effort and scheduling by saying "Let me know when you want to bring someone over so that we can make arrangements for a play date."

You might discover that your daughter wants to interact with younger children as she enjoys social power or the ability to decline and become infantile. They may also note that she is searching for older kids who are introducing her to new things and caring for her. Yet make sure that she also has contact with children of the own generation, as this provides more ways to solve issues relating to sharing and rivalry. And in her classroom, she will have to apply to this age group.

Improving Social Skills of Children with ADHD

During a child's development phase, some skills are quantifiable language skills, math skills, etc.

But what about the softer skills which, like social skills, do not come as naturally? ADHD kids also find it difficult to make friends and establish relationships. Some parents wonder how social skills can be developed, but often don't know where to start.

It is critical for all kids to have positive peer relationships and friendships. However, most children with ADHD have a hard time making friends and being included in the wider group of peers. Oftentimes, the hyperactivity, inattention as well as impulsiveness can disrupt a child's attempt at connecting with the people around them in a positive way. Not feeling belongs, not being accepted, feeling different, isolated, and unlikeable is, unfortunately, the painful feelings children with ADHD go through, and this experience carries on into adulthood, often with lasting and disastrous effects on their future attempts at making friends and forming connections. Children with ADHD are no different than children without all of them want to be liked, want to be part of a group, and want to make friends they just do not know-how. But all is not lost- there are strategies that you can do to help your child develop these social skills and competencies, as we will explore them in this chapter.

Increasing a Child's Social Awareness

According to the various research on ADHD, children with this disorder can be poor monitors of their own social behavior. They often do not have clarity on the awareness or understanding of social situations and the reactions they provoke from people around them. To them, a peer interaction went well, but, or to the other person, it did not. To an ADHD child, an interaction with a peer may have gone well but, it did not. This is another example of an ADHD-related issue, where the ADHD child has the inability to accurately 'read' social situations, self-monitor themselves and adjust their actions and behaviors according to the social setting. These skills would need to be taught directly to them.

Teach Skills Directly and Practice, Practice, Practice

Learning from past experiences also makes it a little harder when it comes to children with ADHD. Often, they react without thinking, but one of the ways to remedy this would be to constantly provide feedback immediately whenever a child's behavior is inappropriate, or they have had social miscues. Role-play is an extremely effective and helpful way of shaping, teaching and practicing positive social skills and providing the child with ways to deal with difficult situations, such as bullying and teasing.

As a parent, you can start by focusing on one or two main areas that your child struggles with the most when it comes to social interactions. This creates a learning process that is not too overwhelming both for the child learning and parent teaching.

Often, children with ADHD have problems with the fundamentals of social exchanges such as:

- Starting and maintaining a conversation
- Interacting with people in a proper way
- Personal distance when talking
- Giving and receiving input
- Listening and asking for ideas
- Taking turns talking in a conversation
- Showing interest
- Negotiating and resolving a conflict
- Speaking using a normal tone.

Identify your child's social rules and behaviors clearly and give them information. Practice these prosocial abilities repeatedly. With immediate rewards, this will form positive behaviors.

Building friendship growth opportunities

For elementary and preschool children, playdates offer a great opportunity for parents to model and coach positive peer interactions for them. For the child, they would be able to practice these new skills. You can set up these playtimes with one or two friends at a time keep it minimal rather than having a large group of friends as this may be overwhelming for the child and for you. Plan playtime to be the most effective for your child.

Consider yourself as your child's "friendship mentor." Consider carefully how long a playdate takes and select activities that are most interesting for your child.

The older the child gets, friendships and peer relationships become more complicated but continue to remain involved in your child's life and help them facilitate interactions that are positive for themselves. For a kid who struggles socially, middle and high school years can be harsh. It would be good if the child can have a least one or two good friends throughout the years of school that can often be the child's support system rather than having a large group of friends.

Socially alienated middle or secondary school students who face constant rejection may feel desperate to become members of any peer group, including those with adverse impact.

Another way to foster positive peer relationships outside of school is to get involved in groups within the community such as Indian Guides, Boy Scouts, Girl Scouts, Girls Who Code, Rotary Club for kids, sports teams, and art groups, for example. When getting your children do join these clubs and teams, ensure that group leaders or mentors know about ADHD and create an environment that is both encouraging and constructive for your child. This is extremely helpful in the long run.

Don't be worried or afraid to share information about your child's condition with kindergarten, coaches, and parents in the community so you know what's going on with your child and who's spending time with your child. Withholding information will only make things worse. The peer group of a child and the features of the group affect the individuals in the group strongly.

Empowering the Peer Status of your Child through School

Peer groups are important for children, but the downside is that once they put a label on your child because of their lack of social skills, it can be hard to break away from this reputation. Having a reputation, especially one that isn't 'cool,' can become obstacles to your child. Negative peer labels are commonly established when the child is in early to middle school and this reputation does not fade away easily, even though the child develops positive social skills. This is one of the main reasons why it is extremely crucial for parents to collaborate with the school and their child's teachers, mentors, and coaches to address any effects.

Lessening or stopping these negatives impacts can be done through establishing a positive working relationship with your child's this is just one such example. Inform them about the strengths and desires of your child as well as what they struggle with. You can also share any approaches that you find helpful in focusing on the areas of weakness of your child.

When forming social preferences about their peers, young children often look to their teacher. A teacher's presence, warmth, acceptance, patience, and gentle direction can be an excellent model for the peer group, and it also has an influence on the child's social status. The teacher plays an important role in finding other ways to draw positivity and positive attention to the ADHD child.

In the presence of the other children in the school, one way to do this is to give the child special roles and obligations. As a teacher, you can make sure that these responsibilities can result in the child feeling success, and this can, in turn, develop feelings of acceptance within the classroom as well as feelings of confidence, self-esteem and self-worth in the self-conscious child.

This also gives opportunities for the peer group to view the child in a positive and encouraging light, which also helps to stop the group process of peer rejection. As mentioned in the previous chapter, it can also help to promote social acceptance by pairing the child with a caring "buddy" in the classroom.

Setting Up Accommodations in School and at Home

The benefits of having a good, working relationship with your child's teacher is enabling them or helping the teacher outfit ADHD techniques and methods in the classroom. This helps the child to better manage their symptoms. Working together with a teacher or an adult caregiver, therapist, or coach on effective approaches towards behavior management and social skills is the best and most practical solution.

Inform your child's teacher about the medication taken by your child and if they need to take it during school hours. Be sure to work closely with the child's doctor as well because you may need to give feedback on your child's responses, symptoms and so on both at home and at school, so the doctor would be able to fine-tune and make adjustments to the child's medication along the way.

ADHD at School Bullying

Insisting on structure in the child's day and having a routine are particularly helpful when your child starts school. Although it has nothing to do with his level of intelligence, your child who has ADHD is most likely to have problem at school. Although ADHD is not technically a learning disability because of their behavioral problem, these children do struggle in the school system. When your child reaches the age of six and starts school, his symptoms become more apparent, and they can also begin to have more of a negative effect on his life. He will have to worry about sitting still and paying attention in a classroom setting as well as remembering and following sometimes complex instructions. He will also have to deal with what is for some children the most difficult of all activities which is interaction with other children in social situations. It also forces the child to wake up early and to learn a whole new morning routine when he probably only just began to master the old one.

Work with the child's teachers and others at the school to help your child in controlling the disorder and getting as much from the school experience as possible. Helping your child to perform well at school is a big part of coping with ADHD in children. In order for your child to flourish at school there must be collaboration between the teachers, school administrators and the parents of the child. Teachers should be well-informed about the child's condition so everyone can be on the same page regarding his needs. Your child will most likely need a great deal of help coping with life at school because he will find it difficult to sit still for long periods of time as school often requires. He may get up and walk around at inappropriate times and says inappropriate things. He may also have difficulty following complex directions needing everything to be explained in the simplest and clearest manner. Parents and teachers should work together to ensure that notes are taken, and homework assignments are completed.

He will also forget to record homework assignment and to prepare for test. Because they aren't always paying attention, they may not know about upcoming activities unless they are written down in his notebook by the teacher. They will be distracted by thing that other student in the class are doing or even thing that are going on outside.

Request and attend meetings at his school with his teachers and school psychologists. Make sure that you are allowed to have input and to ask questions in the meeting. Find out if everyone is moving in the same direction regarding your child's education and if they are not, see what you can do to address the situation. You can also ask for the child's therapist to be present at meetings so that he or she can advise the teachers on the best way to get the most out of their time with the child.

Be prepared to spend many an evening doing homework with your child, who will most likely take a lot longer to complete his homework than the other children in his class and who will need you to help him stay focused and to get rid of distraction.

You should also learn as much as you can about your child's legal rights regarding his education. There are laws in some countries which state that your child cannot be discriminated against for an education because he has a disorder. They also state that provisions should be made for that disorder in the delivery of education, in that if a special education teacher is needed then, one should be provided.

The child will qualify for these special considerations once it is proved that his disorder limits his ability to function at school.

Ask the teacher to keep you informed about what takes place in the classroom, whether your child is being disruptive or not. Getting regular updates keeps you, the parent informed, and able to tell if your child needs further therapy or other types of exercise.

If he isn't already sitting up front, ask the teacher to put him up front where she can tell if he is paying attention and pull him back when he stops and starts daydreaming or gets distracted by something else.

It is also important to let the teachers and school officials know that you have expectations for your child as far as his education is concerned. Make it clear what your goals and objectives are and work with them to achieve them. Get input from the teachers regarding how reasonable those expectations are and welcome their advice and recommendations but be alert for signs that the school has given up on your child and speak to the teachers about it right away. If both teams are not working in tandem, the child will not flourish in that atmosphere.

There should be a special place established where homework is done. Make it a quiet area with no distractions, as children with ADHD are very easily distracted. The television should be off or out of hearing and if there are other children they should be in another room if possible. If you have small children, have the other parent or other family members keep them organized until homework time is over. Make it clear to the child that he must record his homework assignments, as they are likely to forget to do this.

While you will need to help with homework, resist the urge to do it for him, although you might assist by making the instructions simpler so that he can follow them. It might help to divide the assignments into more manageable portions, so your child does not feel overwhelmed. Take breaks if you need to so that he has an opportunity to refocus.

As a parent of a child with ADHD you would probably have to buy extra school supplies such as pens pencils and erasers, because Kids with ADHD tend to forget things and are usually not very organized.

Bullying

While many parents of children with ADHD are teased about their condition at school, research appears to show that children with ADHD are quite likely to become bullies at school. There can be various reasons for this. Because if their inability to fully pay attention and focus on what's going on, the child with ADHD also struggles academically, when you combine all these thing the child must feel a lot of frustration and may choose to show it by bullying other children. Because they do not feel much empathy, they would feel no guilt over taking advantage of another child in an effort to stop feeling bad about themselves and their inability to fit in. Medication would not make a difference in this scenario, as the stimulants usually given to children with ADHD do not weaken the aggression they feel.

Parents can help to decrease or stop the bullying habits of their children by first letting them know in as calm and unemotional a tone as possible that they have been informed about the behavior. Then they have to impress upon their child, who most likely feels no remorse, that while they continue to love him unconditionally, his behavior is unacceptable. Let him know that if the behavior continues there will be consequences just as there have always been for breaches of good behavior. The parent should also work with the child's teacher to try to find something for the child to do at school to occupy his time and give him a sense of responsibility and purpose. He could possibly have a role with one of the sporting teams, tidying up the locker room or do simple clerical tasks for one of the teachers or school administrators. He will feel less need to work off aggression if he is busy completing a task that he knows he has been entrusted to carry out.

Another proactive action would be to try and take him out of the situations where he is likely to bully other children such as during the lunch break or after school. Teachers can ensure that the child spends this time in a location that is supervised. If you want to go closer to the source of the problem, you can sign your child up for counseling or anger management session to teach him to control his emotions before they get to the point of violence, or if you feel you can handle it yourself, you can engage him in role play sessions where you teach him to respond to situations without resorting to bullying.

What you don't want to do when you find out that your child may be bullying, is to lose your temper and scream and shout at your child. Never resort to a violent means of punishment such as spanking because that would just confuse the child because how can you teach that violence is unacceptable by being violent yourself? You do not want to blame yourself either. Your child is not bullying other children because you failed as a parent. Don't react by making excuses for his behavior and finding fault with your own, that would be counterproductive as it would not do anything to alleviate the behavior and will probably make it worse.

Talk to the teachers at his school about what is happening so they can take action, if needed move him out of the situation. Be there for him so he does not lose his self-esteem.

Self Esteem

Children with ADHD are often kept apart from the other children because they are considered disruptive. They might get into fights or be involved in bullying or other kinds of disruptive behavior. Even for events such as birthday parties and other gatherings children with ADHD might be left out because they are in different at a time in their lives when children want to fit in. These exclusions and other forms of rejection can cause children with ADHD to think poorly of themselves and to have low self-esteem. As a parent, it is largely up to you to balance these negative occurrences by praising your child and rewarding them whenever they do well at school or any social situation. It could be for doing something as simple as hanging up his clothes or something more significant such as doing well on a test at school. You have to work with them to achieve small goals.

Apart from praising them for good behavior, let your child know that you love him unconditionally and remind him about everything about him that is good and valuable. Make sure that any criticism of him is constructive and put across in a way that enhances rather than detracts from his self-esteem. Make sure that the criticism is of the behavior and not of him. Don't be too emotional, stay calm. If after repeated attempts, you believe that you are not able to raise your child's self-esteem on your own, don't be afraid of seeking professional help for your child and for you too.

Behavior Therapy

Definitions of psychological therapies for children with ADHD

There are many types of psychological therapies that could be given to individuals with ADHD. The basic therapy forms are cognitive-behavioral therapy (CBT), Social Skills Training, and Family Therapy.

CBT approaches relevant to treating children with ADHD include behavioral therapy, parent training, and cognitive therapy. CBT therapies have been broadly used to boost motor behavior, inattention, and impulsivity of the child. CBT assists children with ADHD to comprehend the connection between their thoughts, feelings, and behaviors. It also teaches them how these interconnections may lead to unhealthy, unsuitable, or maladaptive behavioral tendencies. The second thing CBT aims to achieve in individuals with ADHD is to learn to change their thoughts, feelings, and behaviors and divert them to more positive outcomes.

For this therapy to function effectively, the individual must be ready to practice the changes he or she has identified during the process. Often, CBT therapies join behavioral and cognitive therapies together; however, CBT therapies either involve behavioral or cognitive therapy while working with children. The key psychological therapy for ADHD is presented below:

Behavior Therapy

The major procedure involved in behavior therapy involves using rewards or treats to encourage the child to carry out the desired motor, impulse, or attention control changes. The reward should never be the reason for the change, but it can be a good way of putting a positive impression on the child's mind towards the therapy.

That may include physical rewards like additional time for recreational and leisure activities or purchasing for the child something valuable to him or her.

Another type of reward that is used in behavior therapy includes social appreciation like praise or accomplishment. Great care should be taken when choosing a reward because the reward chosen is specific to that particular individual and must include what the individual is particularly attracted to. A few convenient, monetary, cultural, and moral values should be considered when deciding on a particular reward. Something that would be suitable for some parents may not be suitable for other parents.

Another form of behavior therapy makes use of what is known as negative consequences techniques. These techniques are not used as frequently. Still, this approach is essential when a child's behavior is especially disruptive or offensive to others and should be terminated instantly.

These forms of therapy make use of verbal reprimands. Its advantage is that it is highly functional and very simple to implement by parents, caregivers, or teachers in the school and teaching staff.

The advantage of this is that it teaches kids that there are boundaries. If he or she is rebellious, something will happen. They are not just allowed to do whatever they please.

Another technique employed is the response cost techniques. These involve making the child lose a promising potential reinforce and taking away some of the rewards previously given to the child or an agreed collection of rewards given in progression from which a deduction is made due to improper behavior.

The third form of the technique used in behavior therapy is minimizing the child's time for leisure activities. It usually involves placing the child away from others' attention for a given time to help them get quieter and be more cooperative. If the child fails to co-operate, they are made to go through the same procedure again. Through repeated actions, the child learns when to be quiet and cooperative.

This therapy is employed when it is felt that the child is exhibiting inappropriate, overactive, or impulsive behavior amid parents, siblings, or peers.

Emotional Development in Children

There are many factors that contribute to the emotional development of children. Some are: parents, family, friends, and relationships - parent involvement in a child's life is an important factor in his or her emotional development. This essay discusses how a child's ability to respond with appropriate emotions will help them develop into mature human beings. It also discusses how the inability to cope with stressful situations may lead to more serious problems later in life as well as what parents can do to try and prevent this from happening.

Children who grow up in violent and chaotic environments have trouble in the emotional development process, due to the fact that they never get a chance to practice those skills necessary for them to cope with stressful situations. A child that spends most of his or her time watching a parent abuse drugs or alcohol will have difficulty developing his or her emotional skills because he or she is not getting the guidance from an adult figure. They will also feel as if they are not worthy of attention and as if they are not important to their caregivers. If a child's environment is completely devoid of affection, they can still be affected because they will learn that affection is not important. If a child does not observe enough positive social interactions as a part of his or her development, he or she may have trouble learning how to interact adequately with others.

Children develop empathy and sympathy due both to their own life experiences and by observing and listening to the conversations of their parents. When they observe positive interactions between their parents and friends, children develop an understanding of how relationships should be. When parents demonstrate behaviors that are appropriate and healthy for children, they teach their children that behaviors that are not emotionally healthy for a particular situation will cause harm to them. Children learn how to respond with appropriate emotions by observing how their parents reacted in similar situations. If a child's parents were able to resolve problems without displaying inappropriate emotions, children will learn that it is important to solve problems in the same way. On the other hand, children may see their parents exhibit inappropriate emotions in order to resolve problems and learn that it is okay to respond with inappropriate emotions as a way of overcoming stress.

When children witness their parents experiencing feelings such as rage, anger, sadness, or any other negative emotion, they are able to understand that these are emotions that should be kept private and not shared with anyone. When they observe the same behavior from friends of theirs or peers at school, they therefor can understand how others will react when those emotions become public. They will also learn how to respond to those emotions in the same way their parents did.

Children desperately need a sense of security, which they usually get from the love and support of their family members. Children's emotional development is affected when they feel as if they do not have enough love and support. When children grow up in an environment with too little love, they do not develop an understanding of how they should interact with friends, peers and other adults. Because they do not learn to trust others as they should, they may have trouble later in life if they do not receive the support they need.

Children who are not shown enough love and support at home need to find a way to get it elsewhere. When children do not feel loved by the adults closest to them, they tend to look for love from strangers, who may try and take advantage of them. They may also look for love from someone who is not good enough for them - through crime, drugs, etc. Children need support in their relationships with others; they need to feel as if they can trust their other friends and relatives.

If a child spends all day in the company of one or two other children, he or she may not learn how to handle relationships with others.

If a child does not get enough attention from his or her family members and is also stressed by having too much stimulation, he or she may have trouble developing expected skills when it comes to learning and dealing with stress.

Foods for ADHD Management

To develop recommended nutrition interventions for ADHD, we need to understand the typical eating behaviors of these children. Eating habits were evaluated from structured interviews of parents of boys aged 6 to 10 years old, comparing 100 boys diagnosed with ADHD to 100 boys of the same age without ADHD. None of the children were taking medications for treatment of ADHD symptoms. This research exhibited that ADHD children frequently skip meals more often than the other children, yet they eat more than five times per day in a pattern commonly known as "grazing". Therefore, they eat on a less structured schedule but more consistently. Children with ADHD also consume a lot more of sugar sweetened beverages (SSBs) than the other children, accounting for almost half of daily fluid intake (this means they don't drink very much water or non-caloric beverages). Banaschewski et al5 demonstrated that ADHD children choose the immediate choice when faced with immediate food choices versus delayed food choices. Often, the immediate choices are not the healthy choices.

Anthropometrics

"Anthropometrics" means body measurements – which includes height, weight, head circumference, mid-arm circumference, and lots of other measurements. A person's anthropometric measurements are then compared against reference standards. Children are compared using standardized growth charts; several are available, with the most commonly used ones published by the Centers for Disease Control and Prevention (CDC). These growth charts use actual measurements of thousands of children in the United States of a given age and gender and establish average percentiles.

Growth charts are not the only way that a child should be monitored for nutritional status and health, but they are helpful for forming an overall understanding of their health and nutrition status. Weight status as indicated by BMI for adults is explained in the table. Comparison of their BMI against the average standard using the CDC growth charts can explain the weight status of a child. A child is considered underweight if their body mass index (BMI) for age is less than the 5th percentile. He is considered overweight if the BMI for age is greater than the 85th but less than the 95th percentile, and obese if greater than the 95th percentile BMI/age. Short stature is defined as less than the 3rd percentile height for age. However, serial measurements plotted over time to monitor the trend of the growth is considered to be more important than the actual point on the chart. A snapshot of one of the growth charts is included on the next page, but the CDC website should be used to obtain charts for plotting growth if needed.

Effect of ADHD On Height

By 2005, 29 research papers had been published reporting the trends in growth in height of children using stimulant medications to treat ADHD. This means that children grew about one inch less than expected during the first 3 years of taking stimulant medications (2.54 cm = 1 inch). There was a finite knowledge that rebound growth may be possible if medication use is stopped, meaning that some of the children caught back up on the missed growth once they stopped taking the medication. In 2009, another researcher used more complex anthropometric measurements to investigate whether the slower growth was more strongly correlated to medication regimen of ADHD, or to the disease generally. 52 boys who have ADHD were not treated with medication and 52 boys with ADHD treated with the stimulant medication methylphenidate (aka Ritalin) were compared to the population norm (i.e., the CDC growth charts). Findings suggested that the decreased rate of growth for height may be linked to the disease in general, excluding the treatment with the stimulant medication. In accordance with the former research as evaluated by Dr. Poulton, most children still achieve an acceptable adult height, but this reduction in rate of growth in height should be monitored on a regular basis and addressed if needed.

Effect of ADHD On Weight

It is common among authors that they relate the increase in overweight and obesity to a lower self-control in many lifestyle aspects, including eating-related behaviors. Impulsive children displayed an increased calorie consumption when presented with foods that varied in color, form, taste, and texture. Of note, special testing was conducted to confirm which children were impulsive. The table shows the foods that were used to provide variety, because if you're like me, and you read that impulsive children are more likely to overeat when presented with foods that varied in "color, form, taste, and texture", you want to know which foods those were! Other researchers confirmed that children and adolescents with ADHD tend to eat convenient and easily available foods that are high in fat and sugars4 as they tend to choose the immediate choice5.

Keep all of this in mind for the next portion when we talk about the possible effect of artificial food colorings and sugar sweetened beverages on ADHD.

This fact also promotes the idea that the healthy choice should be the easy and default choice in many food establishments, especially in hospital cafeterias and other healthcare settings.

An example of a "default choice" for healthy eating is when a hospital cafeteria uses a whole grain bun for a grill item unless the customer specifically asks for a white bun, and all pre-made deli sandwiches presented for sale are on whole grain, high fiber breads.

Once these children with ADHD start to take stimulant medications like methylphenidate, they are then actually more at risk of being underweight than overweight or obese.

Stimulant medications are well-known for causing decreased appetite and weight loss.

This may be due to nausea and/or the fact that the medications stimulate neurotransmitter activity in the brain leading to a slow-burn type of "flight or fight" response. This chemical response from the neurotransmitters can lead to decreased appetite. Therefore, children with ADHD who have begun on these treatment regimens have 1.6 times higher odds for being underweight compared to children without ADHD. Tolerance to the medication side effects builds up over time in most people, which means that the appetite will eventually return.

Appetite and Medication Therapy

As tackled earlier, symptoms associated with ADHD can be caused by impaired neurotransmitter activity in the brain and medical treatment for ADHD usually involves treatment with methylphenidate or amphetamine-containing medications to repair this neurotransmitter activity. These medications are well-known appetite suppressants. Some children lose interest in eating altogether or won't eat at certain times of the day, and oral intake decreases significantly.

Sometimes children adjust to the new medications and regain their appetite, but others don't. This can be directed to undesirable weight loss, and if this poor intake continues for several months, it may affect growth in height and lead to micronutrient deficiencies with resulting medical issues. For example, if a child is not eating well and is losing weight, the overall intake of crucial nutrients for growth like iron and calcium is likely to be insufficient.

Therefore, dietitians should help these children and families with nutrition strategies to overcome the suppressed appetite before weight and/or growth are affected.

Lessen oral intake should be tackled with the physician, as medication dosage and timing can be addressed to reduce the effects of appetite suppression. For example, methylphenidate is available in a long-acting formulation meant to be given one time per day, and in a short-acting formulation that is normally given two times per day. If appetite constraint continues for an extended period of time after starting the medication, instead of switching to a new medication, it may help to trial the same medication but in a different dosage or release rate.

If this is not effective, and growth is negatively impacted, it may be necessary to change to a new medication altogether or even stop medication therapy.

Suggestions for shifting food sources and/or supplementation can be done if required.

For other children, overall consumption of calories and protein and fluids may be significantly reduced, making it necessary to develop a more thorough approach to counteracting the effects of the appetite stimulation.

Building Self-Style

We will talk about the essential reinforcements related to ADHD that can help in the improvement of the symptoms of your child. Children suffering from ADHD are always in need of proper support. All that they want is to take the support of others. As they get proper attention from their caregivers, it helps in making them feel soothing besides making them feel better. When ADHD children grow up, everyone around them, including their parents, expect them to abide by some rules and also take care of themselves. Providing an ADHD child with various types of restrictions will never help in solving the problem. You will have to understand all those actions that can help in benefitting your child and also improve their overall behavior. You will have to be aware of all those actions that can actually make their condition worse. As you have proper knowledge of these, along with the reinforcements of the various negative effects of ADHD, you will get the power to reduce all those things.

The primary reinforcements of ADHD have been properly discussed in this section, which might, at times, work in unison along with other types of behaviors to make the symptoms of your child worse.

Accommodation

In most cases, a child will not showcase vigorous behaviors related to ADHD as long as you say 'yes' to them. It is quite normal for the caregivers of the child to provide them with support and comfort the very moment as the child starts whining or creates problems. All such things tend to happen when your child starts showcasing anxiety symptoms, displaying rage, being excessively self-critical or overreacting. Every time a child in any family gets diagnosed with the symptoms of ADHD, the adults of the family try to provide all sort of support to the child. Accommodating an ADHD child might also result in a range of problems.

For instance, when your child is acting out and demanding something so that they can soothe their discomfort, you try to bring that exact thing for him/her. In fact, you will bring the same in large quantities so that he/she does not face the discomfort of any kind. All of this will make your child understand that no matter when they display bad behavior, they will get some stuff that they demand. The symptoms of ADHD have a tendency to flare up as you keep doing more for the betterment of your child and also put in a lot of effort.

Let us have a look at one more common example so that you can understand the problem clearly. When your child is not trying to pay any kind of attention to anything, such as at school or at home, he/she might ask you to properly explain the related matter to them as they were inattentive. Right in this way, they will continue depending on you. The end result of this is that they won't be able to learn self-care for fulfilling their own needs or desires. In case you fail to get your child out of this ADHD cycle and toxic behavior, they might not be able to see progress in any part of their life. The teachers in school will never try to help every student speed up. So, you will have to breed in the values of self-care within your child.

In some cases, a child suffering from ADHD might start correlating rescue with love. It is mainly because whenever they find themselves in some sort of difficult phase or dangerous circumstance in life, you will always try to provide them with the required help and get them out of the situation. However, acts of this kind will make your child feel that if they put themselves in difficult situations, they will be getting all sorts of love from you and thus also be valuable. When an ADHD child is accommodated, you will find that they will keep bombarding you with a series of questions that they either know how to solve or know the answer to. Do you have any idea why? It is primarily because parents always try to leave behind all other important things to answer the questions of their child, and children suffering from ADHD actually prefer this. They intentionally want that you do this for them. Thus, they might try to play dumb or stupid when in actual they are not.

The behavior of this kind often results in assistance from the side of parents as they are aware of not enforcing any kind of conditions on their child or just make them feel accountable. It is your responsibility to provide all sorts of help to your child to overcome their trials. Whenever they are not effective at something, you will have to be there to help them out. Also, your ADHD child might start complaining regarding you not telling them everything. The only reason you are not trying to do so is that you know he/she is not much qualified for all such things. However, things of this sort can easily trigger the symptoms and make them worse.

A self-gratification attitude of toxic nature tends to develop when you start attending to all the needs and worries of your child, even when there is a need to surrender your well-being. In such a case, an ADHD child needs to be pampered at every level. So, they can never come to know about the needs or desires of others. In case you try to accommodate your child, who is suffering from ADHD excessively, along with easements at every single turn to make them achieve their goals, it will result in back lashing later on. So, from the examples and explanations mentioned above, you must have understood that fighting the symptoms of ADHD won't be easy if you just try to accommodate your ADHD child more than the requirement. Let us have a look at some possible reasons behind the habits of over accommodation of parents.

The most common reason why parents try to over accommodate their child is that they feel if nothing is done from their side, their child might face danger. So, the parents of ADHD children always give their best to opt for the safe route as they do not want their suffering child to get hurt in any possible way. They are aware of the potential risks. So, they do not want their kids to get exposed to the same.

Another possible reason is that as shame comes in the way of things, parents can compromise everything very easily. Let me explain this to you with the help of an example. Suppose a couple got divorced and the single mother comes to know that her child is suffering from the symptoms of ADHD. The very next moment, she puts herself in a lot of guilt and shame as she starts blaming herself. She thinks that ADHD came into the picture because of negligence on her part. All of this results in over-accommodating the child in every possible sphere of life. The single mother might also blame herself for being busy with work too much and being unable to take care of her child. However, as we have already debunked this myth, we are not delving into the details again. But always make yourself aware that ADHD never results from bad parenting. It comes with various medical reasons behind it.

A very common reason behind the over accommodation of a child is that the parents might have faced excessive poverty during their childhood. So, when they have a child of their own now, they would not want the child to face the same. So, they try their best to take care of their child in every possible situation and, at times, in a way that can be considered as more than necessary.

The next possible reason might be trauma. Parents try to put in efforts to solve every problem that their child might be facing after trauma. They do so to support their child and so that they do not have to deal with threats of any kind themselves. However, while doing so, they just end up over-accommodating their child.

There are parents who opt for over-accommodation as they do not possess enough time which they can dedicate to their child and help them learn something new on their own. So, they just give in to over-accommodation. They might always be busy because of their schedule at work or because they need to handle a lot of burdens of the family.

So, regardless of the cause of over-accommodation, it is never going to help your child in any possible way. In fact, it might end up hampering the skills of self-management. As a parent, it is quite natural for you to try and make your child's life as easy as possible. However, you will also have to understand that learning to solve problems on your own is a skill that every child requires to progress in life. Just try to think practically. You will not be with your child for your whole life to look after him/her. Indeed, as you help out your child, you will get the chance to develop a new and stronger bond. At the same time, you will be pushing them in the direction of a situation where they might not be able to finish the simplest tasks in life without feedback from your side.

As parents, you will always get a feeling of peace knowing that your child is completely safe with you. However, you will also have to prepare him/her for all those times when you will not be there by their side. So, they will have to learn how to be self-reliant. For example, your child has to complete some project at school, and you are giving your best efforts to make everything simplified for him/her. But you are not actually helping in real. Children need to learn to exert their own selves. Whenever you try to get their tasks done on your own, your child will try to hide behind the same. He/she will never be able to do anything on their own.

When you just keep reminding your child of all those things that need to take or even take all their things yourself so that he/she does not forget them, your child will lose the ability to remember things on their own gradually. It is true that when you try to help your child, it can help in saving a lot of energy and time. In fact, it can also help in simplifying various situations. However, the true fact is that you will not be preparing them for their future. All that you will do is to permit the symptoms of ADHD to sustain.

Attention

The acronym of ADHD is attention deficit hyperactivity disorder. So, the reinforcement that we will discuss in this section is attention. You must have noticed that when you are with your child, and you start conversing with someone affectionately, he/she starts behaving in a furious way. It is mainly because ADHD children tend to feel nervous and threatened when they see their parents sharing any form of an affectionate relationship with someone else other than them. Some of the common actions that can depict this involve your child making weird noises or doing something unacceptable as your attention shifts to someone else. In fact, they might try to target things that are beyond their limits. As your child keeps performing such actions, it is primarily because they want you to attend to them and make you notice what they have actually been up to. At times, you might not even have to talk to someone, but a facial expression of simple nature is enough to trigger such activities.

Examples Of Games for ADHD Children to Find Their Destinations "Cramming Game" Cooling Down Entrepreneurial Game

We're lucky to be growing and thriving in a world of technology that supports our ADHD, not one that shames us for the things we can't control. Though it can still be a daily struggle, managing our ADHD has never been easier will all the friendly technology, apps, and gadgets there are out there.

ADHD-Friendly Alarm Clocks

If you haven't already, you need to invest in an ADHD friendly alarm clock. One of the most popular kinds I've seen are those that actually have wheels, so you have to get up out of bed to turn them off! If you can't afford to buy one like this at the moment, simply moving your alarm clock across the room might help you get out of bed much easier in the morning rather than hitting the snooze over and over again.

There are even alarm clocks that will shoot things across the room that you have to put back in place. Alternatively, free apps on your phone like Alarm will go off and give challenges that you have to complete to make the noise stop!

How this Helps Someone with ADHD

Anyone who suffers from ADHD symptoms will know that irregular sleep is one of the big ones.

Whether you're having trouble getting out of bed because you are lost in a dream, or you're exhausted from a restless sleep and staying up all night due to distraction, it can be very challenging to listen to that first ring of the alarm clock. Using an ADHD friendly alarm clock will help you actually get out of bed and stay out.

There's no mind that can figure things out quite like an ADHD one, however. I've tried a few different alarm systems, but even my groggy mind can find a loophole in some that make it hard for me to get out of bed. Make sure to try your new alarm clock out on a night when you're not totally dependent on getting up at the crack of dawn.

Keyless Locks

Even those that don't struggle with ADHD might find that they are constantly losing their keys. Invest in keyless locks, ones you can open with technology or a code, in order to cut out the stress of losing keys! This will help those with ADHD because you won't have to worry about losing your keys anymore.

Weighted Blankets

Don't forget the important benefits of weighted blankets! One method of making your own is to invest in some scrap fabric and create a quilt. Before sewing it closed, add dry rice to sections at a time, sewing in lines of the rice in order to create a weighted effect. Beware- you cannot wash this homemade blanket!

This is still a good alternative if you're waiting for your weighted blanket in the mail or want to test out this method before committing to it.

Shower Clock

The shower is where I can come up with some of my greatest ideas, but it can also be the place for the most distraction! In order to help me stay on time in the shower, I would listen to music and know after two, three, or four songs (depending on length) that it was time to get out. This helped sometimes, but I would also realize after a few solos and using the shampoo bottle as a microphone in the shower that I was supposed to get out two songs ago. In order to stop this distraction once and for all, I put a shower clock in my tub so that I knew when 10- or 15-minutes had hit so I could actually get out on time.

Don't just use these clocks for the shower, either. Put one in the kitchen when you might be chopping things slowly, or in the living room when you're getting distracted watching TV. While you might think, "I have a clock on my phone," it's not one that's always there. If you can see that it's 1:00, then 1:01, then 1:02 on the clock on your wall, you know it's time to cut things short. You would probably only check the time every couple of minutes on your phone, making you lose chunks of time.

Fidget Toys

Those with ADHD might find that they simply cannot sit still with their hands empty. One great thing to keep around are different small toys, whether it's something that spins, clicks, or is covered in buttons to press.

When you can keep your hands busy, you keep your mind busy and out of trouble. If you look up "fidget toy" on any major site, you will be able to find a plethora of fun little distracting gadgets to choose from.

ADHD Apps

Luckily, we don't have to go to a physical store to get help for our ADHD, just the app store! Some of these are for your browser, other for your phone, and you might even need to pay for some. There are usually free trials or alternatives for most but remember that a few extra dollars can go a long way if it means changing your life for the better.

Freedom

Freedom is an app that will actually block your computer from going online during certain time frames. This is wonderful for me, especially because I would find that I was done with work at 8 P.M. but would often spend my nights mindlessly scrolling the internet until midnight or later.

This will allow you to see when your internet time is going away so you can use it more efficiently.

Mint

I've never been too good with my finances and convincing myself not to purchase anything too massive that is an obvious mistake. Most of my money problems come from small impulses, like ordering delivery just because I don't feel like getting up to make dinner.

Or I might go to the grocery store and get distracted by the sales. Little things like this can add up to a big dent in my finances, so an app like Mint helps me see where my money is coming and going in a way that I understand. It has helped me to stop spending money on things I don't need and actually helped me to save money when I was at a time where I lived paycheck to paycheck.

CogniFit

When I'm bored or feeling anxious, I usually pull out my phone. What ends up happening is that I might get on Facebook or Instagram or one of the seemingly hundred other social media sites I have. With an app like Cognifit, I now have games I can go to and play that won't just be mindless, either - they can actually help increase cognitive function. This is great for those with ADHD because it is a productive distraction that can actually improve your symptoms overall.

ADHD Friendly Tech

Never stop looking for more ADHD friendly tech that you can include in your life. The smallest changes can have the biggest impacts, so don't underestimate the abilities of something you might have heard of that you didn't originally think would help!

Alternative Clocks

We already mentioned shower clocks and different alarm clocks, but you should also think about investing in one that causes you to look at time in a completely different way.

Those that suffer from ADHD have time management issues because of distraction, but also simply sometimes because of the complexities that come along with trying to understand time.

An alternative clock, such as an hourglass, helps you to understand time in a more quantitative way rather than simply watching numbers change digitally. Other clocks might include actual sundials, or things that are similar in concept to hourglasses.

Smart Home Devices

There are so many devices out there that can turn an ordinary home into a place made for those with ADHD. One thing that I absolutely adore is the ability to check my stove, my locks, and that all doors have been closed. These are all done on different apps, but I used to have so many days where I would think, "Did I close the door? Did I turn off the oven?" and the distraction would ruin my workflow. I never forgot to do these things, yet I would always fear that I had. Apps let me check in on my home to make sure that I haven't missed anything, giving me the peace of mind, I need to continue throughout my day.

Online Planners

On any smartphone, you have a calendar. However, it's better to get a different planner that will specifically help us ADHD sufferers. This way, you can plan what you're doing, how much work needs to be done, and plan for time for distractions, as well. Try out a few different calendars at once. You will eventually find one that you go to one more than others, meaning this is your best method! The more you can specify a calendar to your lifestyle, the easier it will be to eliminate distractions.

Alternative Health and Complementary Medicine Food

Traditional Chinese Medicine

Traditional Chinese medicine is one of the oldest complete medical systems on earth. People have been developing and using this system for over 2,000 years. In many parts of the world throughout this period, it was the only health care available. Even now, TCM is used on a daily basis as a basic form of medicine for hundreds of millions of people in China and other parts of Asia.

TCM is often mistakenly believed to consist exclusively of acupuncture. However, it also incorporates a sophisticated, complex approach to herbal medical treatment, as well as bodywork, movement therapy (t'ai chi and qi gong — the latter is pronounced "chee kung"), and dietary prescriptions.

TCM is based on theoretical principles that differ dramatically from those of Western medicine. Describing TCM in these few paragraphs here will give you only an inkling of its complexity and can hardly do it justice. My intention is merely to give you the information you need to decide whether or not you'd like to check into it further and consider it as a possible treatment modality for your child.

In TCM, there are two fundamental concepts: qi or chi (pronounced "chee") and yin/yang. Qi is the vital energy or force that permeates the entire body and mind, and yin/yang refers to the two major principles of the universe whose interaction creates qi and thus all life. In the most simplistic sense, yin refers to female or receptive energy and yang refers to active or male energy.

Disease, according to TCM, has one very basic cause: the disruption of qi energy. If qi is disrupted, disease of some kind occurs. This disruption has three major causes: internal (emotions), external (outside factors such as infection or cold wind), or lifestyle (factors such as poor diet, stress, and lack of sleep). These disruptions create problems in the flow of qi, which in turn throws the opposing yin/yang energies out of balance. All of TCM medical practice is based on restoring the flow of qi and righting these imbalances through acupuncture, herbs, movement, and/or diet.

Acupuncture is the best known of the TCM therapies and the most researched. It restores the flow of qi through energy channels called meridians, which are the means by which qi circulates throughout the entire body to nourish, warm, and protect all cells, organs, and tissues. Energy, or qi, flows up and down these meridians. This energy can be blocked, deficient, or excessive.

These notions of health and healing may sound somewhat foreign to you if not downright strange. Whether or not you accept the theory behind a healing modality, the most important consideration is whether it works. And, as it turns out, there is a sizeable body of research demonstrating that TCM is effective for many conditions.

Ayurveda: An Even Older Traditional Medical System

There is another complete medical system known as Ayurveda, the traditional medical system of India, which is much older than TCM, predating it by 3,000 years or more. Loosely translated as "the science of long life," Ayurveda incorporates dietary, herbal, and life-style therapies in an elegant and complex system that millions of people have used effectively as their single source of medical care for centuries. I have chosen to leave Ayurvedic medicine out of this discussion — not because it isn't effective (it is) for many medical conditions or because it isn't fascinating and full of useful wisdom, but because it is a very complex system, and because relatively few well-trained Ayurvedic practitioners practice in this country.

TCM Research

It's not easy to perform research studies on acupuncture. As with neurofeedback or hypnosis, it's not possible to do a traditional double-blind study as with a medication. People know when they've had needles stuck into their bodies or not! Also, since TCM practitioners don't use the same diagnostic system used in Western medicine — 'yin deficiency' just doesn't translate well into "medicalese" — it is hard to replicate traditional acupuncture practice in a Western study. Despite these obstacles, enough research has been done to show that TCM is effective for a number of medical conditions.

Since 1996, over 7,000 articles have been published about TCM, and most (over 5,000) were published in English. Much of this research was performed in conventional research settings.

For example, a medical group called The Cochrane Review had this to say about acupuncture for chronic tension headache, a medical condition that is very difficult to treat: "The authors conclude that acupuncture could be a valuable non-pharmacological tool in patients with frequent episodic or chronic tension-type headaches."While this may not sound like an unequivocal endorsement of acupuncture, it is actually a very strong statement given that the Cochrane group requires any treatment to meet very demanding standards before stating that it is effective.

Here is a short list of diseases, symptoms, or conditions for which acupuncture has been shown to be effective in at least some controlled clinical trials, as compiled by the World Health Organization (WHO):

- Adverse reactions to radiation therapy and/or chemotherapy
- Biliary colic (cramping caused by gallstones)
- Correction of malposition of fetus (for example, a baby that is breech, or upside-down, in the mother's uterus) or for induction of labor
- Dental pain
- Depression
- Dysentery (diarrheal disease caused by the shigella bacterium)
- Facial pain (including pain caused by temporomandibular joint dysfunction, or TMJ)
- Headache

- Hypertension (high blood pressure)
- Hypotension (low blood pressure)
- Knee pain
- Leukopenia (abnormally low white blood cell count)
- Low back pain
- Menstrual pain
- Morning sickness
- Nausea and vomiting
- Neck pain
- Postoperative pain
- Renal colic (kidney pain)
- Rheumatoid arthritis
- Runny nose caused by allergy (including hay fever)
- Sciatica
- Shoulder pain caused by arthritis
- Sprain
- Stomach pain (in peptic ulcer, acute and chronic gastritis, and spasm of the stomach wall)
- Stroke
- Tennis elbow

Thus, there is little doubt that acupuncture can be an effective treatment modality for many conditions. You may have noticed that ADHD is missing from this list, however.

Unfortunately, only limited research has been performed about TCM for treatment of ADHD. Only three randomized studies have been reported. One study showed that electroacupuncture and behavioral therapy were more effective for ADHD than "sham" acupuncture plus behavioral therapy. This required six treatments per week for 12 weeks.It's hard to imagine treatment ever happening at this intensity level in the U.S. or any other western country!

According to Dr. Bob Flaws, a leading Western expert on TCM, ADHD has only recently been recognized in China. Dr. Flaws notes that interest and research in ADHD surged in China in 2003 — perhaps, he speculated, due to the adoption of Western food and lifestyle. There could have been a true increase in the number of children developing ADHD or just an increased focus on previously unrecognized children who exhibited symptoms of ADHD.

In translations of seven recent articles on the treatment of ADHD with acupuncture or herbal medicine, Dr. Flaws reports consistently positive results. However, the studies have a number of limitations. None of them had an adequate control group, there is no randomization, and some of the results are so dramatically positive as to defy belief. I think all one could reasonably say is that these studies indicate that TCM could be an effective treatment method for ADHD but higher quality research needs to be done to prove it.

Here is an interesting story from one of my patients. Her son had Asperger's syndrome as well as attention issues, and had developed disturbing involuntary, obsessive movements of his fingers.

You saw my son G, who was diagnosed with Asperger's syndrome. I wanted to report the positive results we received from acupuncture with Dr. C. G had involuntary movement of his fingers. He touched his fingers to each other over 100 times a minute. He did this almost non-stop. He had this involuntary movement for almost six months before the acupuncture started. G did not experience any involuntary movement while he was actually receiving acupuncture. After each visit, it took longer and longer for him to revert back into the involuntary movement. His frequency became less and less after each visit. After four weeks, there was no involuntary movement at all. Nothing else changed for G during this time he received acupuncture. He had been on fish oil and zinc for six months when he started acupuncture. G had the acupuncture with Dr. C twice a week for six weeks. Then, G received follow-up acupuncture once a week for almost a year. The involuntary movement has not returned. I credit the involuntary movement cure to acupuncture. G also reports feelings of calm and wellbeing from acupuncture.

The Chinese Medicine Perspective on ADHD

Although this particular information is not necessary to know to receive treatment, you might share my fascination with the way in which Chinese medicine looks at this disorder. According to the TCM perspective, the main symptoms of attention deficit hyperactivity disorder correspond to the traditional Chinese disease categories of irritability (yi nu, duo nu), insomnia (bu mian), profuse dreams (duo meng), oppressive ghost dreams (meng yan), vexation and agitation (fan zao), and impaired memory (jian wang). According to Flaws' translation of a Chinese medical text on the subject, "The main disease mechanism of ADHD is the presence of some sort of heat evils which harass and stir (dong) the heart spirit." Imagine the part about vexation, agitation, and harassment rings a bell with some of you!

Is TCM Safe?

Acupuncture is very safe. Any responsible practitioner uses new, sterile needles each time, eliminating danger of contamination. The incidence of complications from acupuncture is extremely low. For smaller children who don't like needles, acupressure or other non-needle methods can be used.

Chinese herbal medicine may not be as safe. As mentioned in Chapter 9, contamination has been an issue with a number of Chinese herbal preparations. Some were found to contain lead; others, pharmaceutical additives that would produce the effects the herb was supposed to produce. Some Chinese herbal creams for eczema, for example, have been found to contain steroids — the pharmaceutical treatment for eczema. Sticking with the most reliable Chinese herbal companies — those that observe strict standards of safety — is the best way to avoid this problem.

The herbs' long tradition of use is a good indicator of safety, but there is at present some unavoidable risk involved.

The Bottom Line on Traditional Chinese Medicine for ADHD

Overall, I would recommend the use of acupuncture for any child with ADHD if previous interventions have not solved the problem, especially when the only other choice appears to be pharmaceutical medication. The risks are low, it is not overly expensive — some insurance plans even cover it — and a few sessions should be enough to indicate whether continuing the treatment is worthwhile. On the other hand, I cannot recommend Chinese herbal medicine across the board for children with ADHD because of safety issues. It could be used on an individual basis with the guidance of a trusted practitioner, especially if treatment was confined to herbs with known safety profiles.

Finding a Good TCM Practitioner

Acupuncture has become an extremely popular treatment modality in the United States. It is practiced by two main groups: (1) acupuncturists whose medical training has been entirely devoted to traditional Chinese medicine, either in China or in the United States; or (2) Western medical doctors who have added acupuncture to their qualifications through coursework and practical training. The most respected courses require over 300 hours of the trainee's time.

Understanding Children with ADHD

Kids diagnosed with ADHD are often told they can't do anything without taking medication, but science has shown that this isn't the truth. The condition is often misunderstood, too: there's more to it than just hyperactivity and inattention. Many people with ADHD have additional difficulties, and it's vital to find a practitioner who is familiar with that particular presentation of the condition.

Not only does understanding ADHD help mitigate some of the difficulty, it also helps you gauge how your child is doing on his or her medication regimen and what else you might need to help them manage symptoms. It's a huge step toward helping them feel better about their abilities while living up to their potential.

Executive Functioning Deficits in Children with ADHD

One of the first clinical psychologists to study ADHD, Russell Barkley, has said that the executive functions (self-control, working memory, planning ahead) are often behind the hyperactive-impulsive symptoms. While it's true that generally poor executive functioning is an indicator for ADHD diagnosis in adults and children alike, many people with ADHD have executive function difficulties beyond those related directly to hyperactive-impulsive symptoms.

Inattention isn't always disorganized or procrastination—sometimes it's just a lack of follow-through or organization skills. It can also be a result of an overstimulated nervous system. That's why it's so important to get an evaluation early on if you feel your child isn't functioning at the level he or she should be. If your child is struggling in school, low grades are one sign that executive function deficits are impacting his or her ability to do well.

Are You Getting a Complete Picture of ADHD?

Overstimulation and under stimulation both affect executive functions, which means that overstimulation can lead to inattention and underemployment of brain resources. Understimulation can also impact attention and work ethic if it doesn't lead to enough effort in response to the under-arousal, or relaxation response, associated with being bored.

Identifying ADHD is a process, and not everyone is helped by medication alone. In these cases, it's vital to have all of the tools you need to help your child succeed, which means knowing about his or her particular presentation and getting a complete assessment. The evaluation should include not only psychiatric interviews and questionnaires but also neuropsychological testing that can provide information about attention problems related to under- or overstimulation.

Understand Different Types of ADHD Presentations

ADHD must be diagnosed by a professional in order to receive appropriate treatment, but some practitioners are better at finding accurate diagnoses than others. Many of these professionals are referred to as "experts" rather than psychologists, but that doesn't mean they aren't trained in validating ADHD as a legitimate condition. There are several different types of ADHD presentations that can affect executive function and response to medication, and there's more to the condition than just hyperactivity and impulsivity.

ADHD with Overactivity: Hyperactive-Impulsive Symptoms

Many people who have ADHD have hyperactive-impulsive symptoms that cause inattention as well. It's a common presentation that can cause considerable underachievement in school, and it often leads to social problems as well.

Inattention is one of the most common symptoms of ADHD in adults, but people with hyperactive-impulsive symptoms also have problems concentrating and planning ahead. This means they're often less likely to get through college or complete work at a high level, and it can result in difficulty getting a job that is more than cleaning or serving customers.

Many people with these symptoms have an endless amount of energy but may lack the ability to focus on one thing for long enough to get anything done. A person with ADHD may be adept at cleaning a room, but if the task is boring or too taxing, he or she will get distracted and move onto something else.

Getting the right treatment can help with symptoms and help people with ADHD learn to differentiate tasks that require more concentration from those that don't. While medication can be effective for hyperactivity and impulsivity, talking therapies can help with inattention as well.

ADHD with Underemployment: Inattention

The symptoms of inattention can look a lot like the symptom of underachievement. The difference is one of degree.

For example, a child may be able to answer questions in class and volunteer to answer them correctly, but she might not understand them or know how to apply the information that she's learning. She may be able to do her homework without any help and even get all of her assignments finished on time, but they might be incomplete or poorly done. This is often due to either a cognitive problem or an overreaction to stress—or both.

A child who has ADHD will need to have this addressed in order to succeed in school, though medication might be helpful with the underlying symptoms of impulsivity and hyperactivity.

ADHD with Disorganization: Proactive Symptoms, Inattention, and Underemployment

Proactive symptoms show up as problems with starting tasks or finishing them properly. You might notice that your child doesn't seem to know where things are in his or her room or wallet, or he or she might have trouble getting out the door on time. This can result in frustration and a sense of failure that spreads to other areas of life and can keep a person from succeeding socially as well as academically.

Being disorganized can also impact people's emotions. Organization can help people manage their time and plan for the day ahead. This leads to a cycle of failure and poor self-esteem, which makes it difficult for those with disorganization issues to find success in anything they do.

Many people who struggle with organization have trouble focusing on one thing for very long because there are always too many things to look at or worry about. It's important to keep your attention focused on one task and get that finished before moving onto something else.

If your child is struggling with these symptoms, it's important to talk to him or her about his or her thoughts and feelings. Asking questions like "What are you thinking about right now?" can help your child learn about his or her own thought process. This can help you help them break the cycle of failure, disorganization, and stress that is keeping them from succeeding in school or gaining a higher level of education than their current situation would seem to warrant.

Does ADHD Ever Go Away?

Ah, the joys of having ADHD. You know it's a laundry list of obstacles: social stigma, economic difficulty, inability to focus on anything for long periods of time... The list goes on and on. But you're not alone! In fact, about 10% of children in North America have this condition; there's no need to feel weird about it anymore.

And the good news is that yes, ADHD can go away. It's not a lifelong curse, and it's not a death sentence. The bad news? It can take time.

Adults with ADHD have trouble with focus, organization, time management, and impulse control... And the disorder is marked by hyperactivity in childhood and a tendency toward inattention when they're older. Adults who have grown up with the effects of this disorder often struggle to deal with it; for some people, it's debilitating in relationships and career paths.

But, like we said before, ADHD can go away. That's the good news.

It also takes patience — you probably won't see results overnight. (Although you might be surprised by how much things change.) But it is worth the effort.

ADHD is not a death sentence, and it doesn't mean your child cannot be successful. Educate yourself about the disorder and reach out to your local mental health organizations for more information. And don't forget to ask your doctor! The best way to understand a disorder like this is by getting the professional input that you need. ADHD can be managed with the correct treatment; when you seek help, you can eliminate the challenges that this condition brings about. It's worth it in the end — so take care of yourself today!

Parents and ADHD Children

Attention Deficit Hyperactivity Disorder, or ADHD is the most common neurological disorder in children. It's a chronic condition that begins in childhood and often continues into adulthood.

Parents with a child who has ADHD often feel overwhelmed or frustrated by their inability to manage the situation on their own, as well as guilty about not being able to provide adequate care because of this lack of knowledge. The ADHD parent may feel as though they are not in control and frustrated that their child is not following directions, seems to be in constant motion, or does not listen. Parents with an ADHD child may feel guilty about the situation because they recognize that aspects of their own behavior resemble those of their child.

Children may become agitated or have difficulty focusing when certain people attempt to correct them or discipline them because it clashes with how their brain is wired. They become very active when confronted by a simple task or directive that appears dull and uninteresting, such as homework, washing dishes, or taking out trash. This is because their brain chemistry is different than that of a typical child. They may not seem to understand why they are being corrected or punished, and they may become disinterested in the task at hand, resulting in their behavior worsening.

Despite these difficulties, ADHD should not be misdiagnosed as a severe disorder. Most children diagnosed with ADHD will grow into healthy adults with stable mental health and job skills. However, some children who are diagnosed with ADHD do develop more severe symptoms in adulthood; other than this rare occurrence, it is very unlikely for any child to experience long-term significant problems during childhood or adolescence related to ADHD.

The National Institute of Mental Health (NIMH) has found that the disorder is more prevalent among males than females, but more girls are being diagnosed. ADHD is seen in children of all races and ethnicities, as well as children from a variety of socioeconomic classes, including those who are living in poverty and those who are wealthy. Children with ADHD may be diagnosed at any age.

Children with ADHD tend to act out early in life and often have difficulty forming attachments to others as well. They may have difficulty paying attention or making decisions, which can get them into trouble with their teachers, bullies, or other authority figures very early on. Even though they may appear to be acting younger than their age, they are actually several years younger.

The symptoms of ADHD are not part of a severe brain disorder as was once thought. Instead, it is now known that the symptoms of ADHD are related to how the brain functions. While treatment for children with ADHD is usually medication and behavioral therapy, the greatest success comes from finding ways to help the child develop successful habits and skills in areas of his or her interest so that he or she can attain a sense of comfort and confidence in those areas. After all, continued achievement can help bring about meaning to life and improve self-confidence, which helps pave the way for more meaningful relationships with others later on.

Parents of ADHD children often do not know where to turn for help. The more parents learn about ADHD, the better able they are to help their child learn skills necessary to cope with the disorder.

When seeking out information about ADHD, parents should look for evidence-based sources such as national institutes for mental health or universities that may have additional information. Parents should not rely on people who sell products for ADHD or doctors who may not be well-versed in the disorder.

Parents will be faced with challenges while raising an ADHD child. It is important that parents find support from others who are facing similar challenges and understand how to best help their children thrive. This can be a tough task, but one that is very worthwhile and gratifying. Most importantly, it is critical for parents to know that they are not alone in their struggles to help their children succeed.

ADHD is characterized by short attention span, impulsivity, and hyperactivity. Some people have just one symptom while others may have all three of these issues to a varying degree. Affecting approximately 2-5% of school-aged children and 4-9% of adults worldwide, ADHD can sometimes be managed through life style changes such as getting enough exercise or eating better. Often times medication is needed to manage ADHD.

Though it is not known why ADHD develops in some people, there are many theories. One of the most common theories is that it may be due to a problem with dopamine in the brain, which causes people with ADHD to have difficulties with attention and regulating emotions.

People with ADHD may have trouble performing tasks that rely on sustained focus and concentration for long periods of time, such as spelling, or following verbal directions. People with ADHD may have difficulty paying attention to details and repeatedly doing the same things over and over again without errors or interruptions. These changes are called disorganization and are typical of people with ADHD.

These challenges are often mild, and the disorder is often diagnosed only after problems in school or on the job become apparent.

Other symptoms include impulsive behavior (e.g., blurting out answers to questions before they've been completed), hyperactivity (e.g., fidgeting, running about), and high levels of anxiety or restlessness (e.g., difficulty playing quietly). Some individuals with ADHD may also have low levels of motivation and diminished self-esteem, although it is not clear whether these are related to ADHD itself or other factors such as family problems, peer pressure, low self-discipline, poor education, or unemployment.

Because people with ADHD have problems in these areas, they often show difficulty coping with everyday life. However, ADHD is not a mental disorder and most people with ADHD are not mentally ill. People who have ADHD may be highly sensitive to criticism and may become anxious when facing tasks that they know are difficult for them, such as doing schoolwork or filling out job applications.

At times, the symptoms of ADHD cause enough trouble and dysfunction that it affects a person's ability to function in social relationships or at work. In children, this may lead to poor performance in school and problems getting along with parents or teachers. In adults, the symptoms may lead to relationship problems and trouble at work.

Experts used to believe that many children outgrew ADHD as they grew older; however, there is now more evidence supporting that ADHD is a disorder that lasts a lifetime. Moreover, according to the Diagnostic and Statistical Manual of Mental Disorders (DSM-IV-TR), ADHD often lasts into adulthood and occurs in more than 70% of those affected by it.

People with ADHD tend to have problems in the following areas:

1. Inattention – Difficulty staying focused and paying attention to details; often makes careless mistakes; has difficulty following instructions or completing tasks; and has difficulty sustaining attention during tasks or activities.

2. Impulsivity – Acts before thinking, often in risky situations; interrupts conversations or others' activities; blurts out answers before questions are finished.

3. Hyperactivity – Fidgets or squirms a lot (e.g., unable to stay seated); runs about (e.g. unable to stay seated at school); cannot play or take part in leisure activities quietly (e.g., talks too much or blurts out answers before questions are completed).

4. For the most part, people with ADHD tend to have problems with anger, aggression, and conflicts in relationships as a result of the disorder. These problems may be more severe in children than adults.

The prognosis for children and adults is the same: Most people with ADHD will grow out of their symptoms by adolescence. However, many adults continue to have some symptoms; some even have a form of ADHD that lasts into adulthood.

Diagnosing ADHD in adults can be complicated because some of their symptoms may appear to be symptoms common to other mental health conditions, and because changes throughout an adult's life can affect how they present.

How to Live with an ADHD Child

If you have a child with ADHD, you may feel like your days are full, but your life is empty. You've come to the right place for help! We'll show you how to adjust your expectations and style of parenting in order to stop feeling overwhelmed and enjoy life with your child again.

1. Educate yourself!

As a parent of a child with ADHD, it is important that you understand the condition and how it differs from other types of learning disabilities and behavioral problems. It is essential that as a parent you learn as much as possible about how this condition impacts your child's life and what can be done to help them overcome their difficulties.

2. Set realistic expectations.

You may feel overwhelmed by the situation to the point that your life revolves entirely around your child's problems. Do you want to continue working? Are there things you no longer enjoy? What do you want to do instead? What will it take to make these changes, and how will they benefit both you and your child? Only when we are willing to make changes in our lifestyles can we begin living a fulfilling life again.

3. Make time for yourself.

Your child's difficulties may make it feel like you have no time for yourself. This is a recipe for disaster because you are bound to become resentful and eventually this resentment will come out in your relationship with your child. Make time for activities that are important to you.

4. Make time for your partner and family members.

Having a child with a disability can put a strain on families and relationships, particularly when there is a lack of support in the home. Remember that family members also need time to complain about the situation, so encourage them to talk things over with you.

5. Get help from other sources of support:

Support groups and therapists can be helpful for both you and your child. Children love to develop friendships with other kids who are dealing with similar problems, and they tend to be more comfortable around people with disabilities. Therapists can point you in the direction of other therapists and teachers who understand your child's condition. They can also help you set up meeting times with those professionals.

6. Develop a strategy for emotional support:

If anything, as children with ADHD get older, they tend to get more focused and creative about ways to cope with their difficulties.

7. Don't let your child's behavior control you:

Children with ADHD will test your limits from time to time, and it is important that you don't allow their behavior to control you or the household. This means setting firm boundaries and sticking to them. Set up a reward system for positive behavior so that kids with ADHD know what will happen if they misbehave. It also helps to mediate anger before it boils over, so that your child doesn't hit out in response to feeling hurt. Praise them for taking their medicine and teaching them how it makes them feel better.

8. Take care of yourself:

If you are feeling low or overwhelmed, it is important that you do something to lift your spirits, whether it is going on a walk, going to a movie or spending time with friends. Remember that no child can be responsible for making you feel bad; if your life is truly being filled with worry and stress, then take control of your situation and make some changes.

9. Don't let the kids run the house:

At the same time, make sure no one is punished simply because they have ADHD tendencies (i.e. no one should get a spanking for being late for dinner and then be yelled at, or punished, for forgetting to take their medicine).

If you are struggling with your child's ADD or ADHD, it is important that you seek the help of a professional. Your child can benefit greatly from specialized treatment, and the earlier they receive it the better. A doctor will be able to provide you with information about resources in your area that might help you get the help your family needs. You can also find books at lulu.com that will give you some ideas on parenting strategies for children with ADD/ADHD.

ADHD Skills and Development

How to Improve His Personal Skills?

If you have children who are struggling with ADHD, then these eight tips for how to improve their personal skills might be of some help.

1. Help them control their reactions and emotions
2. Create a calm and positive environment
3. Set clear expectations for behavior and consequences for misbehavior
4. Foster good decision-making skills through repetition of desired behaviors over time
5. Teach them self-regulation techniques that may include deep breathing or relaxation techniques
6. Help them set aside their different learning styles
7. Assure them that hard work and perseverance are the keys to success
8. Work with them on their academic studies and test taking skills.

The word attention deficit hyperactivity disorder (ADHD) is made up of three main characteristics of a person which are:

- Inattentiveness
- Hyperactivity
- Impulsivity.

A person who has the above-mentioned facts would be suffering from Attention Deficit Hyperactivity Disorder. This cannot be cured but can be controlled by medications and with behavioral therapies, which have been successful in alleviating the symptoms. The psychological and social development of an ADHD child will depend on his family's awareness about the attention disorder along with their support and understanding to help them cope up with it. Parents should also understand that their child is not going through a phase rather it is a permanent one. They should interact more with their children and give them more attention than they usually give.

ADHD is a developmental disorder which appears in the childhood to form during the younger years of life. Most cases of ADHD are mild and respond to behavioral interventions including the use of medications, while some have severe symptoms which require specialized treatment programs.

Inattentiveness- Inattentiveness is when a person does not pay attention to what they are doing or what's going on around them even if the activity takes an immense effort like reading, writing etc. ADHD children tend to spend more time daydreaming, daydreaming, fidgeting with things or not attending to their surroundings.

Hyperactivity- Hyperactivity is the over activity of a person. They do not stop what they are doing even when there are distractions and even if there are other people around them. ADHD children can be seen running around without any sense of purpose or talking non sequiturs in the middle of a conversation. They have trouble waiting for their turn in games and activities, calling out instructions or directions etc.

Impulsivity- Impulsivity is when a person does something impulsively without taking the time to think it through before deciding on an action or behavior. The thing that an ADHD child does impulsively is usually done without taking control, which may be harmful to themselves or others. This also includes not having patience to wait in a line, getting angry with others and being impatient for their needs.

ADHD children tend to not play well with others, finish their schoolwork/homework on time and have trouble deciding on what they should do next during the day. They often do things that are not constructive such as play fight with their siblings, hit themselves, have temper tantrums and hit others without any reason. They also have trouble paying attention in class, finishing their assigned work etc.

ADHD has many symptoms reflecting in the individual's and his family's life. These continue to grow throughout the course of a child's life. The earlier a child receives proper treatment for ADHD or worsens and persists with their symptoms, the more serious it gets and becomes especially if they fail to receive treatment for this disability. Parental support and an understanding of ADHD is required to help children cope up with it successfully, so that they can control their behavior and make the most out of each day.

Creating a calm and positive environment at home helps them to be less confused about what they should do next and how they should react to situations or around people. It also gives parents an opportunity to get closer to their children in order to gain trust from them, as trust plays an extremely significant role in providing effective treatment to ADHD children.

Knowing what is expected from your child is very crucial for living peacefully with them. Without clear expectations, they cannot tell the difference between right and wrong and what behaviors are expected of them. It may help parents to create a "contract" of what they expect from their children. This will actually assist them in teaching their child how to get along with them in whatever way they can.

This will also help them understand how people react differently from each other when faced with similar situations or problems concerning themselves.

Being a calm and positive caregiver also includes taking charge of their social skills, emotional intelligence and their behaviors at school and at home. The parents are responsible for knowing what is going on with them through the day. They are also supposed to communicate with the teacher so that they can have effective treatment for ADHD so as to be rid of it for good, if the symptoms persist throughout the life span.

Parents who treat their child's ADHD as a real disability rather than an inconvenience make a great impact on their lives. They understand that children have rights too, like any other human being, which should be respected by all members of society without any discrimination whether it is based on race, gender, age or income level.

ADHD treatment is never the same for everyone. Thus, some children have more difficulty coping up with their symptoms than others. These include activities like painting an inspirational picture for a child that has learning difficulties or runs out of the classroom while listening to their teacher, writing letters to your children's teacher and their friends, giving them different tasks every day and providing them different activities for them to be involved in.

All parents would like to know how they can help raise healthy and independent children who are able to function well in society, without experiencing any disabilities, as they grow up into adults.

It is actually very important to create a positive learning environment at home, in partnership with the teachers who teaches your child, so that they can maintain their self-esteem. Trying alternative treatment for ADHD like a non-medicinal approach can help them deal with their disabilities faster. Talking to them about their disabilities and how they are going to overcome it can also be a big help since they may have been struggling with it for such a long time and probably feel embarrassed when others know about ADHD.

Helping them be more focused on their goals in life is actually what will keep them motivated to become better as time goes by.

How to Teach Social Skills

Social skills are incredibly important, for everyone. There are many children with ADHD who struggle with learning social skills because they often have difficulty focusing on the task at hand. However, there are plenty of ways that you can teach social skills to children with ADHD at home. Here is a list of just some of the techniques that you can use to help your child build better social skills and get along better in the classroom:

-Physical activity increases brain blood flow and improving focus, mood, and memory which is necessary for learning social skills. These activities can go from as simple as taking walks around your neighborhood to more difficult tasks like playing golf or soccer. These activities do not have to be done alone, however. You can have your son or daughter take part in these activities with friends or siblings.

-Playdates are a great way for your child to learn how to make friends. Through playing with other children of the same age, children with ADHD can learn how to interact and play positively with kids their own age. While having your child host his or her own playdate may seem difficult, there are plenty of ways you can help out. For example, you can help your son pick out the games that he wants to play and even let him choose who they invite over.

Play to your child's strengths. Children with ADHD have minds that work differently than others and this can cause them to be frustrated, especially when they are trying to learn. If you have a child who is good at sports, allow them some time after school or on the weekends to play a sport. If your child has trouble sitting still, provide them with an activity that requires more movement such as playing catch or even running around in a safe area inside or outside of the home.

Teach your child positive ways of working through frustrations and negative emotions like anger and frustration. These feelings are very common in children with ADHD because they have trouble focusing on their goals and staying centered during difficult tasks. Try to help them understand that these feelings will pass and that there are better ways of dealing with their frustrations.

Encourage your child to avoid blame. When a child with ADHD loses focus, rather than placing blame on yourself or other people, look at the advantages of what you can learn from your mistakes. In time, you will be able to learn how to handle your ADHD while having fun and doing something that is meaningful for you as a whole person.

The key to learning social skills is practice! Children with ADHD tend to have trouble remembering instructions or following through because they often have short attention spans. However, children who practice these skills often will get better at them in the future with consistent practice over time.

Medication is the first thing that most parents will think of when it comes to helping their children with ADHD. While these medications do help, there are often side-effects that can greatly impact the way that your child operates throughout his or her daily life. While these medications can be useful, it is more beneficial for your child to learn social skills rather than depend on medication for their everyday life.

However, there are plenty of ways that you can help your child build better social skills and get along better in the classroom.

How to Help Develop Empathy and Self-Control

There are many causes of ADHD, but the most common is that children with ADHD have trouble emotionally regulating themselves. Empathy, which lets you understand and share the feelings of others, is a key component in regulating emotions. Children with ADHD may be able to learn empathy skills through sensory training or rewards-based learning activities like games and crafts — two other types of therapy for people with ADHD. Parents can also help their kids develop empathy by making sure that they recognize their child's behaviors as "evidence," which will let them know when their child feels overwhelmed or anxious.

Parents can help their children with ADHD learn to recognize their feelings by using a variety of resources. Make sure that your child sees a doctor to evaluate his or her symptoms and develop a treatment plan, but also make sure your child is familiar with some common emotions and how they show up in typical or atypical ways in children with ADHD.

Step 1: Teach Your Child Basic Emotions

It's easy for parents to think that the hard parts of raising an ADHD child are social skills training, which just isn't true. Having social skills is just like having a second language. It's difficult to learn, but once you pick it up, it's just there.

Step 2: Identify Emotions in Yourself and Your Child

Relate by giving examples, for instance, "My husband has social anxiety disorder, so I have a pretty good sense of what that looks like. "I can look at him and know 'It's that time of day' or 'It's been a tough week. You need a pep talk.'"

Step 3: Help Your Child Identify Emotions in Others

When you see another person feeling a certain way, explain to your child what that emotion looks like and how others might be processing it. If you're out in public and see someone crying, point out that they look sad. Talk about how their tears or slumped shoulders let us know that they're upset about something.

Step 4: Give Your Child an "Emotional Reading"

When Kids Don't Understand ADHD is different from disorders that affect thinking, such as autism or intellectual disabilities. That means your child's behavior isn't necessarily difficult to read. But it also means that ADHD parents may have a harder time communicating with each other and understanding each other's feelings. If you speak the same language, you understand each other much better. If one parent is calling the child a brat, and another parent is saying he's just being childish, they might not be getting at the problem. Parents can learn to read their children's emotions by breaking down what an ADHD child feels and looks like into simple descriptions of true or false. Repeat these descriptions aloud so your child can get familiar with them. Offer your explanations at family occasions like bath time, mealtime or bedtime story time.

Step 5: Teach Your Child to Recognize Emotions in Others

In addition to talking to your child about emotions, you can also help him or her recognize them in others. Help your child identify the various 'emotion cues' that are universal across cultures, such as a frown, tightened lips and clenched jaws. You can have fun with your child learning how other people express their feelings, too. People say that children with ADHD don't understand emotions. But they think about empathy. They know that other people might be sad, but they don't know what that means.

By teaching your child to recognize emotions, you can support the emotional regulation skills that are often impaired in children with ADHD.

Step 6: Make Sure Your Child Understands

How He or She Makes Others Feel When you feel overloaded and anxious, it can be difficult to put those feelings into words or think of things to say to make them better. Don't worry if your child doesn't notice that others are feeling overwhelmed. Children with ADHD understand much more than they're able to communicate. They get overwhelmed by life and have bad days all the time. They just don't always know what to do about it. If your child takes a long time to express how he or she is feeling, make sure he or she understands that other people might be uncomfortable, too. Your child may have a hard time accepting that others don't want to be around her. It's important for parents to explain this and model it.

Step 7: Help Your Child Prepare for Social Situations

Make sure you're also familiar with the social rules that govern when people are allowed to make eye contact, shake hands or speak in public — all ways we communicate our opinions and feelings. When your child gets to kindergarten or first grade, take him or her to a normal class and let him or her observe other children. Make sure your child watches how the teacher talks to the children. They'll see that the teachers say things like 'It's time for lunch,' but they don't move their facial muscles.

Step 8: Make Social Contextual Information Available

Parents can't know what their child is thinking unless they're there with them, and they can't predict how other people will act if they're not present. But we know that context can make a big difference in how we interpret information and respond to situations. When you're in a store and you see everyone around you wearing black, you know it's a funeral. When your child talks to someone, he or she might not realize that if they made a mistake it could be very embarrassing.

You can provide your child with contextual information about social situations by explaining why other people act the way they do. Tell your child that when someone is mad at them, they might look angry or cross their arms and turn their back. When your child is in a group of peers, ask him or her to describe what the other kids are doing and feeling. You can also ask someone else to tell your child what they're thinking or feeling.

Step 9: Help Your Child Understand How His or Her Actions Affect Others

It's important for your child to develop a sense of empathy — the ability to recognize that other people have emotions and think things — but even more essential is the ability to understand how your child's behavior affects others. Parents need to teach their children that they are not in control of how they are about to be treated. The power shifts between people all the time.

If you're with your child and he or she does something that hurts someone else, make sure you ask why. Your child may not pick up on this, which is why it's so important that they learn these skills.

Studies have shown that when parents ask their child why they did something and tell them how it affects the other person, kids are much less likely to do it again.

Step 10: Help Your Child Understand How His or her Actions Can Hurt Him- or Herself

Many children don't want to explain themselves because they feel like they're going to be judged. But if you expect your child to explain his or her behavior, you must be able to listen, too. Give your child a chance to explain what he or she was trying to do so that you can help him or her understand that when people don't like how we're acting; we might not get the response we want.

Children who are sensitive to feedback might begin to tune out after they get a certain number of "no's." If it seems like your child has stopped listening and isn't letting you have an impact, back off for a minute. Be patient as you continue to try to help your child understand how his or her actions affect others.

Step 11: Emphasize That Your Child Is Ultimately Responsible for His or Her Own Actions

Because young children often don't understand that someone else is upset until they're told, parents can take the responsibility for making sure their child knows how their behavior affects others. Once your child understands what he or she did that made someone else mad, you might suggest that he or she apologize. But let your child know that he or she is ultimately responsible for how he or she behaves.

Step 12: Avoid Blaming Yourself for Your Child's Behavior

Now that you understand more about why children act the way they do, it can be easy to blame yourself if your child has difficulty getting along with others. But this can be detrimental for child development because it can lead to low self-esteem. Instead, try to understand why your child acts the way he or she does and deal with his or her behavior from that point.

Step 13: Work Together with Your Child

Once you've managed a child's behavior adequately, it's important to work together as a family so that everyone understands what is expected of each member and how their behavior affects everyone else. You can also make sure that each family member has an opportunity to talk about what he or she does well and what they could do differently in the future.

Establish simple guidelines for behavior. Share the ground rules with your child. This might include charting points in a notebook, allowing him time-outs in his room, or writing a note to someone he may have hurt.

Don't make threats unless you will follow through on them. "If you are going to take another piece of cake, I will take away the toy I gave you last week" is a much more effective threat than "if you do that again, I am going to spank you."

Get support from your family and others who care about your child's well-being. If your child has ADHD, you might find it helpful to talk to other parents who have ADHD children. Ask for their advice or encouragement and possibly ask them to check in on your child's behavior with you.

When it's time for your child to leave home, he or she needs friends individually who understand his/her situation. Remind him/her that lunch is a one-on-one experience and that he/she should not take responsibility for the actions of others, such as when they are eating on the table in front of them at lunch time. Essentially, this means no one should take responsibility for his/her own actions unless they have agreed beforehand to do so.

Pros And Cons of Being ADHD

As ADHD grows in prevalence, so does the stigma surround it. Many think it means students are lazy or stupid. Even some adults think they can trick a doctor into giving them a diagnosis so they can get stimulants for studying and become better at work. ADHD is frustrating – but not as difficult as being misunderstood. The following discusses the pros and cons of having ADHD: from being hyperactive to staying at home all day, from being unable to focus to loving anything new and exciting, from quickly getting bored in school to excelling with difficult tasks, from never finishing homework assignments to living life on the high-octane side without even trying.

Hyperactivity

The most obvious pro of having ADHD is that there is a lot of energy to do things. Many ADHD students are very social and popular. They are the leaders in clubs and other extracurricular activities such as sports, music, and drama. They may be the class clowns, but they also raise group morale with their enthusiasm.

Many people like working out at the gym because it makes them feel good about themselves to get stronger and look better. ADHD students can have this same experience by taking advantage of their energy to make their lives more productive, fun, and enjoyable.

Attention Deficit Hyperactivity Disorder, or ADHD, is a neurobiological condition that makes it difficult for people to pay attention and learn new information – two things it is necessary in life. There are many ways to be good at both paying attention and learning. Some people might have an easier time than others with these issues, but no one is truly "bad" at them. Students with ADHD can use their hyperactivity to their advantage by choosing activities that will help them become better learners and more successful students overall.

Staying Home All Day

Many kids with ADHD never go to school at all because they are either homeschooled or not in the public school system until they are a high school senior or later. They may not be interested in traditional schooling. They sometimes have difficult relationships with their parents, teachers, and school officials because they disagree about how to deal with their absences from school. In addition, some families cannot afford the time and money that is necessary to homeschool a child who has ADHD.

These kids are called "school phobic" but this just means that they do not want to go to school because it does not work for them or their families.

In some cases, the school officials themselves might be part of the problem by not being able to handle their ADHD students. This disorder is very frustrating for everyone involved, especially teachers who are forced to deal with these difficult students and families who are trying to meet their needs.

Not Getting Bored at School

Some people with ADHD can go through the same information over and over again like a tape playing in a VCR. They can hear the same lecture or read the same story so many times that they become bored. Other people may think about one thing for hours but never get around to doing it because they have too many ideas and never have time before they need to do something else. They are always thinking about something else instead of the task at hand.

People with ADHD are often very good at multi-tasking and getting more things done in a shorter amount of time. They can use their attention deficit to get caught up on all their papers and homework at once. They can go from one thing to another without stopping because they never get bored. They don't need to spend hours focused on one thing because they are able to spread out their study time over many days or weeks until it is done.

Advantages of ADHD

Because people with ADHD seem to be able to accomplish more than others it makes sense that they might have certain advantages over other people who do not have this condition.

The Pros:

- Being able to see more details at once.
- Being able to hear more sounds at once.
- Being able to respond to many situations quickly.

Being able to multitask better than others. With ADHD, there are many things going on in a person's brain all at the same time but individuals with this disorder are rarely distracted by extraneous thoughts or other things around them that keep them from focusing on what they need to do.

Being able to learn faster

Being able to memorize information quicker. People with ADHD are often more aware of the words or numbers they are trying to remember. They focus on what they are supposed to have learned and they follow through on their studies and assignments quickly and efficiently. They do not get distracted by extraneous ideas or other thoughts.

Being able to work harder than other people when it comes to studying, sports and other creative pursuits.

- Having a mind that constantly needs stimulation

- Having a quick mental process that can think outside the box and solve problems quickly

- Being able to get lost in your own world and explore your imagination

The Cons

- The tendency for people with ADHD to be easily bored and need something new or a change of pace all the time

- Procrastination because you are easily distracted by other things when you should really focus on one task at a time, such as reading an article or finishing homework. This can cause school grades to drop.

- Lack of self-control in activities like watching TV, eating, or spending too much time on social media sites.

- You might be missing important details in a lecture or social situations due to mental confusion.

- The inability to stay on task at work, school, or in relationships. You could lose out on learning opportunities or opportunities for friendship because you find it difficult to focus well when others are talking.

- The inability to follow through with plans and projects that you make. You jump from one idea to the next without finishing a project before moving onto another one.

- Can become easily overwhelmed when writing long essays, reading textbooks, completing tests, listening to lectures in school or lectures about complex topics like psychology or history.

- A person with ADHD might be easily distracted by people around you. They are also easily bored if they do not have many stimuli such as conversations or an interesting TV show to watch.

- People with ADHD can become negative, sarcastic, and impatient in social situations that require patience or understanding.

- People with ADHD often have a short attention span, especially when it comes to reading something lengthy like a book or study material at school; this makes it difficult for them to learn the material they read because their mind is so full of incoming information from other things that are happening around them.

- You might have a hard time reading social or emotional cues, such as seeing how someone is feeling; you might misread people's emotions and feel like you are being attacked if they are upset with you.

- Can become easily bored and distracted in your daily routine. The monotony of a regular life can be extremely difficult for someone with ADHD which makes it hard to complete regular tasks like homework, chores, or cleaning the house.

- You may find yourself making mistakes in schoolwork or at work over and over again simply because you didn't focus long enough to see how to complete the task correctly.

- Most people with ADHD have a lower self-esteem than their neurotypical counterparts. This is because of the low self-esteem that comes with constantly feeling frustrated with yourself because you can't complete what you need to get done. The other reasons for this are the feelings of inadequacy and frustration that can often arise in social situations.

- People with ADHD often have a hard time relaxing and enjoying leisure time activities because their mind is always going 100 miles a minute. Even when they are not doing anything, they have trouble being still and letting their mind slow down.

- This inability to relax and enjoy leisure time or spend time with loved ones can make it difficult for you in relationships as well as friendships because people without ADHD might become frustrated by your inability to slow down and do things at regular speed.

- Attention Deficit Disorder can often cause relationship issues with people you live with or family members because you are inclined to be more negative, impatient, and sarcastic than your family members might like.

- You might have a hard time understanding the emotions of others even if you aren't just being sarcastic or negative. This inability to read social cues or understand the emotions of others could lead to problems in romantic relationships because it is not only difficult for someone with ADHD to stay focused on one thing at a time, but it is also difficult for them to be patient and UNDERSTAND what their partner needs in a relationship.

- The inability to focus and the need for constant stimulation can lead to you having a negative outlook on life. You might think that there is nothing good in life or that everything sucks and that you're going to have a terrible day, even though it might be the opposite.

- People with ADHD may feel as though they are more special than other people because they are so different. This can lead them to internalizing this feeling of uniqueness as being better or smarter than others which can cause serious self-esteem issues even if many people think of them as "special" or "intellectual.

Children with ADHD may also have other learning disabilities.

When people are diagnosed with ADHD at a young age, they start out being taught coping strategies and self-management techniques in order to help them deal more effectively with the disorder. One of the easiest ways for these individuals to learn how cope with these issues is by using a list of things that they need to do or look at while they are engaged in some specific activity. It is very easy for someone who has ADHD to forget what they are supposed to be doing so often it helps if they have an aide reminding them what needs done. This list serves as a way for the person to stay focused on what they are doing. If one step of the process is done, then it helps them remember that they need to go to the next step or do something afterward.

Therapy and Cure for ADHD

Attention deficit hyperactivity disorder (ADHD) is a type of mental disorder characterized by problems with inattention, hyperactivity and impulsiveness. ADHD affects an estimated 6-7% of children, making it the most commonly diagnosed childhood disorder. In recent years, scientists have made significant progress in understanding how the brain works and what factors contribute to ADHD symptoms. However, because there are no drugs or medications that can cure or treat ADHD, therapists and parents often turn to alternative methods of treatment to manage its symptoms.

The therapy

Behavioral therapy is the most common form of therapy used to treat ADHD in children. It helps them to better control their behavior and eventually stay organized, focused and on-task. In behavioral therapy, children learn how to improve their self-management skills at home and at school. They also learn ways to deal with their impulses and how to make better decisions when faced with difficult situations. Research has shown that behavioral therapy is one of the most effective methods for treating ADHD in children.

The drugs

A stimulant drug like Ritalin or Adderall can improve symptoms of ADHD by increasing levels of the neurotransmitter's dopamine and norepinephrine in the brain. These medications work by increasing the release of these chemicals from nerve tissue. Many parents worry that a child will lose weight if they use these drugs to treat ADHD. In fact, some children who take stimulant medications may actually gain weight as they become more active and less sedentary. The stimulant drugs are not designed to cure ADHD; instead, they are used in combination with behavioral therapy to treat symptoms associated with the disorder.

The surgery

Cingulotomy is a surgical procedure that blocks areas of the brain's frontal lobes that regulate behavior and behavior control. This procedure is currently used to treat repetitive behavior, such as the compulsive behavior that some children with ADHD display. The surgery involves a surgeon inserting a burr into the frontal lobe. This technique enables the surgeon to limit activity in the area of the frontal lobes so that it can't cause unwanted behaviors. Other forms of neurostimulation have also been used in some parts of the world for treating ADHD, including deep brain stimulation and transcranial magnetic stimulation. These procedures involve placing electrodes or coils inside of certain regions of the brain to control certain symptoms associated with ADHD.

The alternative therapies

Many parents find that alternative therapy is more effective than behavioral therapy or drug treatment for controlling symptoms of ADHD in children. Alternative therapies include dietary changes, vitamins and supplements, homeopathy, Ayurveda and herbal medicine. Experts believe that several of these alternative treatments actually work by increasing the brain's neurotransmitters and inducing certain chemicals in the brain.

Synthetic diets

One popular alternative treatment for ADHD is a synthetic diet, which has been used in more than 50 countries around the world to treat children with ADHD. This diet restricts certain types of foods that commonly cause allergic reactions in people who suffer from ADHD. The theory is that reducing intake of these allergens will reduce or eliminate allergic reactions and other symptoms associated with ADHD. This diet requires parents to feed their children an extremely limited list of allowed foods (e.g. celery, zucchini, bananas, oatmeal and rice) for a few weeks or months. As the restrictions are gradually lifted, parents can slowly introduce more foods into their child's diet. A study conducted in Italy reports that nutritional supplements are effective in treating ADHD symptoms of children who have low levels of certain vitamin and mineral nutrients involved in normal brain function. These deficiencies impair neurotransmitter function and can cause symptoms of ADHD.

An Ayurvedic approach

Ayurvedic medicine is an alternative treatment designed to restore healthy states of mind and body. In India, it has been used for thousands of years to treat a wide variety of medical conditions including mild depression, anxiety disorders and attention deficit hyperactivity disorder (ADHD). Ayurvedic medicine uses herbs and natural products to promote detoxification of the body and mind. The goal is to balance the autonomic nervous system, which controls automatic functions such as breathing, heart rate and digestion. The approach encourages healthy eating habits that include minimal gastric acidity and a diet free from excessively cold foods and spices.

Homeopathic remedies

Homeopaths believe that symptoms of ADHD can be treated by giving patients natural products that contain trace amounts of substances that cause ADHD in healthy people. Homeopathic remedies help to stimulate healthy neurophysiology by stimulating neurotransmitters in the brain.

Vitamin supplements

Supplementation with certain vitamins can be a useful treatment for ADHD in children who are deficient in specific nutrients. Deficiency of vitamin B6 and zinc, for example, has been linked to symptoms of inattention. Experts recommend using a multivitamin that contains vitamins B6 and zinc.

An herbal formula

Kapha is one type of Ayurvedic formula that can be used as a natural remedy for managing ADHD symptoms in children. It is believed to have a calming and sedative-like effect on the body. Kapha helps to balance the Vata dosha, which controls movement and emotions. The formula is made up of eleven herbs including Brahmi (Centella asiatica), Shankhapushpi (Convolvulus pluricaulis) and Vacha (Acorus calamus). These herbs are believed to have anti-stimulant and calming effects that can help children with ADHD.

Kapha is best given to children who suffer from anxiety, restlessness and hyperactivity. It is also recommended for children whose ADHD symptoms are associated with physical excesses or suppressed emotions. These symptoms include having high blood pressure, a fast pulse rate or slow digestion.

A combination of homeopathic remedies and Ayurvedic herbal formulas has been successful in controlling the symptoms of ADHD in many children who don't respond well to behavioral therapy or drug treatment. A team of experts may be needed to help parents select the right alternative treatment for their child's ADHD symptoms and recommend the best regimen for them.

Methods in Dealing with ADHD

Many of us are familiar with the onset of ADHD, as it is a common disorder amongst children, teens, and adults. Many people find themselves struggling to deal with these symptoms in adulthood. Rather than accepting the symptoms as a part of their personality for life, there are ways to suppress these characteristics and live well with this condition. In fact, here are 9 methods on how to deal with ADHD.

1. Identify your weaknesses

First, it is important to identify what your weaknesses are in dealing with these symptoms that come from ADHD. You may not realize that you may be unable to deal with situations that make you angry or highly emotional. These issues may be related to your ADHD but can also be a result of the stress and emotional challenges of everyday life. By identifying these weak points, you can then get help from someone who will help you combat these weaknesses. There are ways to do this such as joining a support group or learning more about the condition and its effects on everyday life.

2. Check your emotions

If you find yourself being overly emotional, this is a common side effect of ADHD as well as other disorders. If you find yourself having trouble managing your emotions, it is best to seek the help of a counselor or psychiatrist. For those who have ADHD and are in need of medication, there are several options available such as Ritalin, Adderall, Focalin XR, Strattera, Vyvanse etc.

3. Try other medications

If you have tried several different medications and have not seen the effects needed to control your ADHD, it is best to visit a psychiatrist or neurologist who can help prescribe the right medication. You may also want to try new methods of dealing with your symptoms such as going for a run, meditating, or getting a massage.

4. Reach out for support

Because ADHD can make it difficult to cope with everyday life, it is important that you reach out for support from friends and family members who understand what you are going through. Some places where you may find support are online forums that focus on this disorder as well as join a local support group.

5. Lifestyle changes

One major lifestyle change you can make that may work well for your daily surroundings is to save more money for paying the bills. You may want to think of other ways on how to save money or increase your income by doing new activities or learning new skills. If you find yourself spending a lot of time online, this can be a problem as well as using more money on video games and other activities that do not provide a lot of value in return. This can be a problem, but there are ways to rectify this. For example, meditating, exercising, and reading can all help you find more time in your day that will help you deal with this disorder.

6. Think strategically

When it comes to dealing with ADHD symptoms, it is always best to think strategically on what works and what does not. Thinking strategically about the progression of your symptoms when trying to change them into something positive can be difficult. This could result in emotions doing the wrong things such as going into overdrive or remaining strong and stable while ignoring your thoughts and feelings at a later date. The best advice you can take from here is to learn how to control and suppress the symptoms of ADHD with a strategy. All methods for handling ADHD should be put into action as a result of thinking strategically about ways to deal with ADHD.

7. Whatever works for you

Whatever method you choose for dealing with ADHD should work well for you in your everyday life. If going out more often or getting more sleep does not help in your daily routine, then it is best not to think about changing the way you handle your symptoms as they may last longer than expected or leave lasting effects in your life, such as resentment on other people over working hard to get rid of the symptoms only to have them return later on.

8. Ignoring ADHD

If you have ADHD symptoms and you do not want to take any action in dealing with them, it is best that you just ignore the symptoms. You may want to play a video game, watch TV or movies, or read a book and just ignore the symptoms as they are not going out of your way in dealing with the disorder. You should also be present without worrying about certain situations and events that may make you angry or overwhelmed. The best advice to you is to work hard on yourself in order to suppress your ADHD symptoms as much as possible in order for them to become less powerful over time.

9. Sleep

You can do this by finding activities that help you feel more refreshed such as going for a walk or taking a nap in the afternoon. The worst thing you can do is ignore these symptoms and let them take over your life without any control over them.

10. Medication

Although some people do not want to take medications for instance, they can be considered helpful in dealing with ADHD symptoms. An online search can provide information on medication that you may be interested in taking. Although it is important that you consult a physician before taking medication for ADHD, some of these medications are even used to induce desired results such as increasing sleep or cognitive functioning in order to deal with ADHD using different methods than taking medication by itself.

11. Support

It is important that you have support from people who understand how you feel in dealing with your ADHD symptoms. The support of others can give you encouragement when you are working hard in order to change your daily routine. This can help you deal with stress, depression, and anxiety over time including the symptoms of ADHD that may affect the way you deal with life on a daily basis.

ADHD Coaching Tips for Parents

1. The common areas of concern for parents include paying attention to homework and chores, remembering appointments and special days/dates (i.e. birthday, anniversary, etc.), being on time for special events, or

sports/activities, remembering other people's birthdays/special days/dates (i.e. friends), and getting along with family members and friends.

2. Make a doctor's appointment to check your child's vision and hearing as these can be easily overlooked but are easily correctable issues that can cause symptoms of ADHD-like behavior.

3. Consider hiring a coach to provide one-on-one coaching for your child if he/she is having difficulty in school. Some schools offer this service free; if not, you should look into private coaching or tutoring services that can help your child succeed in the classroom.

4. If your child is having difficulty in school, you may need to consider private tutoring or private school for your child if the problems are severe enough to affect their ability to succeed in the classroom and this can be compensated for with homework tutoring services or possibly by hiring an after-school tutor.

Most symptoms of ADHD can be treated using medication, behavioral therapy, exercise, and lifestyle changes that will help improve overall functioning of the brain as an individual with ADHD so they can live a more productive life in all aspects rather than being stuck in perpetual ADHD mode.

Importance Of Dealing with ADHD

A common misconception about attention deficit hyperactivity disorder is that it's just a misdiagnosis. However, those who live with ADHD know that it's a very real condition with tangible effects on their lives. While there are many possible treatment options, those dealing with ADHD usually resort to medication.

It can help promote better academic performance and increased focus in studying and working. It provides long-term benefits such as avoiding substance abuse or driving accidents among other negative consequences. Further, the sooner you seek treatment for

ADHD the less likely your symptoms will continue to worsen over time or cause children to fail academically or socially in school.

Attention Deficit Hyperactivity Disorder (ADHD) is a brain-based condition that affects the person's ability to concentrate and focus. It's characterized by the following symptoms: hyperactivity, inattentiveness, impulsivity, and restlessness. People with ADHD can find it difficult to stay still and have difficulty controlling impulsive behavior. They do not always follow through on tasks and may spend too much time fidgeting or daydreaming. Adults with ADHD tend to be less productive at work because of poor concentration skills and are more prone to procrastination than those who do not have this condition.

When children are diagnosed with ADHD, they may need to undergo a series of tests, such as brain scans and blood tests, to confirm the diagnosis. In particular, what is the importance of dealing with ADHD?

Some people may wonder why it's necessary for parents and educators to seek treatment for ADHD; however, their lives can be considerably better if they do so. The benefits of working toward achieving a diagnosis include:

Better Academic Performance and Increased Focus in Studying and Working: People who have been diagnosed with ADHD tend to perform better academically than those who do not have this condition. Specifically, ADHD patients that have been treated are more likely to graduate from high school and earn a college degree. With treatment, children with ADHD will have less trouble focusing in class and are less distracted by external stimuli than their counterparts who do not have this condition.

Long-Term Benefits of Avoiding Substance Abuse: It's common for people with untreated ADHD to turn toward substance abuse as a means of self-medicating symptoms in order to cope with the day-to-day activities. However, those who have received treatment are far less likely to abuse substances than those who do not have this condition and don't seek help for it. Not only does medication address the ADHD symptoms and hyperactivity, but it can also help reduce anxiety and aggression. Parents should be aware that stimulants used to treat ADHD may also raise the risk of addiction in some individuals. Without treatment, there is always a chance that children, teens, or adults with ADHD will develop an addiction to substances as they attempt to manage their symptoms on their own.

It Provides Long-Term Benefits: According to the National Institute of Health (NIH), early intervention with treatment for ADHD can result in long-term benefits. Specifically, those children who have received treatment are less likely than those who do not have this condition to repeat a grade or drop out of school completely. ADHD treatment may also result in improved academic performance, better social skills for children, and improved family relationships. These long-term advantages can be beneficial to the person's future by helping improve their career prospects and overall health.

How Soon Should You Seek Treatment for ADHD? The short answer is: the sooner the better. Children who are diagnosed as having ADHD are more likely to be successful in school as well as later in life if they receive treatment early. The NIH has found that the longer a child goes without medical attention for ADHD, the more severe his symptoms will become over time and his ability to function in social situations will worsen. Many adults who have attention deficit hyperactivity disorder do not seek treatment because they believe that their "behavior" does not make an impact on other people. However, as mentioned, untreated ADHD children are more likely to drop out of school and fail to graduate, which can negatively impact their future prospects.

In order to confirm a diagnosis of ADHD, your family physician may refer you to a specialist for additional tests if necessary.

Managing ADHD

If you have ADHD, you probably know all about the struggles. Managing time is difficult, remembering things is hard, and the constant feeling of "noise" in your head gets tiring as hell. For starters, take a deep breath and relax — just because one characteristic might be frustrating doesn't mean that every aspect of your life has to be a chore. You're just another person who has to work harder than others in certain aspects. Knowing how to cope with ADHD is the first step to overcoming it.

Here, you will find some ways that you can manage your life with ADHD and make the most of it. Take what works for you and leave the rest; there are thousands of opinions out there, but only one that works for you.

1. Get enough sleep!

ADHD medications are typically taken in the morning to help someone focus throughout the day, but not getting enough sleep can be a big problem for someone suffering from ADHD as well. The key to getting the right amount of sleep can be as simple as going to bed at the same time every night and waking up at the same time every morning. But if you don't have a consistent routine in place, try to get into a routine where you go to bed and wake up at the same times every day.

2. Stay organized!

A big part of having ADHD is having disorganization. This results in a lot of things going missing, but if you have an idea where everything is in your house, you'll be able to save yourself a lot of anxiety and stress. The key to staying organized is making it easy for yourself; for example, keep all toiletries in one place so that you don't spend valuable time looking for them. You can also purchase storage containers that are conveniently labeled. This will help you find what you need quickly when the time comes.

3. Reduce distractions!

People with ADHD usually find themselves distracted easily, especially at work or school. You can reduce these distractions by turning off the television, keeping yourself away from your phone, and not going on social media while you're trying to do homework or work. If you need to get something done for work or school, make sure that you have a dedicated space where you can sit and focus. This will block out any potential distractions that are in your way.

4. Keep a cleaning schedule!

If you struggle with ADHD and cleaning in the same vein, this one is for you. Keeping a cleaning schedule is going to be essential if this is an issue with you, as it will make everything much easier to handle when it comes time to clean up the house. The key to a cleaning schedule is to set aside specific times of the day for cleaning up; for example, you can have a time where everything is cleaned up around 3 p.m., another on Mondays, and another on Wednesdays. This way, everything will be done in a logical order so that there's no chance of going off track or forgetting about your tasks.

5. Bring on the coffee!

Caffeine is a great medication for any person suffering from ADHD, so why not take full advantage? Caffeine has antidepressant properties as well as improves wakefulness and focus. That means adding caffeine to your daily routine can do wonders for how you feel. The key to keeping up with your normal coffee intake, however, is trying to observe a balance between coffee and soda. Drinking too much caffeine at one time will make you jittery and anxious, which isn't good for anyone who has ADHD.

ADHD treatments are getting better and better each year, and there are tons of ways for you to use this stuff without having to take medication every day. With this in mind, there are many things that you can do on your own in order to manage ADHD symptoms whenever they come up. Remember that this isn't going to be the same for everyone because what works for one person might not work for another. So try out these methods and see how they work; if nothing else, it's good to know that there are things you can do on your own in order to make your life a little easier.

Conclusion

People with ADHD should also learn how the condition can affect them differently depending on what age they are and at what stage in their development they were diagnosed with ADHD. This will discuss why understanding the different developmental stages can be so important for people living with a diagnosis of ADHD.

The ADHD brain develops differently from the brains of those who do not have it, and this difference can be seen across a person's lifespan. In fact, some experts believe that there are three different stages of development in someone who has ADHD: childhood (or childhood onset), adolescence, and adulthood. The symptoms as well as how they affect a person will differ based on which stage the individual is in.

For example, depending on when the individual received their diagnosis of ADHD and who they were interacting with at the time, they may have experienced a more or less stressful environment. This in turn could affect how their ADHD symptoms manifest themselves.

It is also important to understand that the symptoms of ADHD can be very different in adolescents versus adults. For instance, one study found that over 80% of high scholars who met the criteria for ADHD did not meet clinical criteria for it when they were older. It is important to consider this information when deciding whether it is appropriate to treat someone with ADHD with medication at an early age.

Adults living with adult onset ADHD will often experience sleep problems as well as a loss of focus on one's work or studies. These are two conditions that are not commonly seen in adolescents. In fact, it may be more appropriate for adolescents to be treated first with a non-stimulant medication (such as Strattera or Intune), which will help to calm them down and improve their ability to focus.

A common problem for adults who live with ADHD is that they may struggle with anxiety or depression due to the effects of living with the disorder. People should be aware that there are many different treatments available for these issues, including ones that can be combined successfully with ADHD medication.

Because the symptoms of ADHD are so varied across individuals, it is important for those who live with the condition to find out as much as they can about it in order to improve their quality of life. It is also important to understand that, regardless of what medications one may choose, ADHD is not something that is self-medicated. A diagnosis should always be individualized by a professional because medication will not cure or heal a person's condition; it will only play a small role in how effective treatment may be.

Learning as much as you possibly can about the disorder and starting treatment early is an important step in this process. It also helps to find new things that you enjoy doing that may help you feel better about yourself.

It's important to remember that receiving a diagnosis of ADHD does not mean that your life will be worse off than those who do not have it. Instead, it is a call to action in which you can learn new ways of coping with the condition and lead the life you were meant to have.

One minute you feel like the world is on your shoulders, and the next minute you feel like you can do anything. But one thing remains true: life will be hectic; there will always be battles to fight, but it does get easier over time. This offers some tips for those raising children with attention deficit disorder and an explanation as to why this disorder is often misdiagnosed as ADD or even depression. So, if things seem tough now, know that they will improve — just give them time.

The biggest concern a parent of a child with ADHD might have is whether they will be able to give the child a good education. However, as a parent, you can lead your child on this path by employing these tips:

Help Your Child Focus in School

For Example:

Make sure your children are well rested. If they're tired, they will struggle to concentrate on their studies. It's important to schedule time for sleep and wake them up when it's time for school.

Protect them from distraction and interruptions by putting away phones and shut off the television so that your children can focus on doing well in school.

Give your child a theme to follow when doing schoolwork each day. Perhaps they can color in a picture of their theme — like shape or animals — or write information about it in their notebook. Their ADHD makes it more difficult for them to focus on one topic at a time, so help organize what they need to do.

Give them toys that require concentration as well as play-doh and other materials that allow for creative outlets. These will help tremendously!

Make sure your children get plenty of omega 3 fatty acids by eating fish, yogurt, beans, nuts and seeds frequently (or by taking supplements). Omega-3 fatty acids will improve concentration and reduce hyperactivity and distraction.

Give them omega-3 fatty acids and exercise at the same time. For example, walking to school will reduce hyperactivity and improve concentration, and supplementing with omega-3 fatty acids will help their memory.

Omega-6 fatty acids (such as hydrogenated oils, fried foods and meat) cause ADHD. Avoid these foods as much as possible!

Let your children use a computer for their homework, but never a cell phone or tablet because these devices are highly disruptive.

Make sure your children do their homework when they're fresh. This could include schoolwork, playing outside, or a nap.

Teach your children to use deep breathing exercises to control their stress and help them focus on what they need to accomplish.

Give your children rewards that are very specific and be sure that they have earned those rewards (otherwise, the system won't work).

Create a chart for school completion that shows how many days it took for them to complete their work and how long it took them to complete each item. This will help you better understand how long it takes your child to get things done in order to better manage expectations.

Give Your Child a Journal

This has been an invaluable tool for parents of children with ADHD. You can create a special journal for them to record their daily history and note what type of attention they need to receive from you. When they're older, you can show them this journal and ask them how they felt as a child (perhaps they will think back and have fond memories of the times when you listened). It will help your child understand their strengths and weaknesses as an adult. If they didn't get enough attention in school, maybe now is the time to give it to them.

Include your child in the solution. Let your children know that they have ADHD, but that doesn't mean there isn't a way to help them.

Have Fun with Your Child

Learn how to play tag and other fun games with your child; not only will it be fun, but it will also teach him/her sportsmanship and how to win graciously (which is very important). ADHD children will often lose their cool if they don't win and can think that the world is out to get them. Having fun playing games with your children will show that you want to be a part of their lives.

Tell them, "You're doing a great job helping me around the house" or "I love how kind you are." Show up at your child's sporting events and support him/her emotionally; ADHD kids are emotional beings because they're so sensitive and easily hurt (especially by rejection).

Don't just say "No" when your child asks for something. Their frontal lobes are underdeveloped, so they won't be able to understand why you said no. Instead, tell them what you will do with your child in place of the long-awaited vacation. For example, "Instead of going to the beach, we'll go on a hike through Tilden Park."

Give Your Child Life Skills

Help your children develop some life skills that they can use in the future. Learn how to bake bread together and show them how fun and delicious making food is. Teach them about car maintenance or how to repair things around the house; not only will these help them as adults, but it will also teach them patience and responsibility (so that one day they can have their own homes).

If you have an idea for something that you want your child to do but they're not cooperating, try saying "What do you think?" instead of "You need to..." This is a great way to get them to listen and feel like they're part of the solution.

Do Your Best to Understand Your Child

Be patient and be understanding. For example, if your son doesn't seem to understand why you told him he had to come home after school, try doing some research. Ask them what they think would happen and how it could help them in the future. Then ask them how much they wish their mother would help them figure out how to get a good education.

This is the main problem with ADHD children; whatever we teach our kids in school is not going to stick forever. Our children forget the information they were taught in school very quickly, so trying to force our kids to learn things that are not readily available to them will only make them resentful. It's better for them to learn these life skills through trial and error, which is how we all learned. Hopefully this all helps some parents out there.

WOMEN WITH ADHD

How to Overcome the Hidden Struggles of Living with ADHD. Embrace Neurodiversity and Learn the Best Emotional Control Strategies Thanks to the Power of Self-Discipline

Mary Jane Goals

WOMEN WITH

ADHD

How to Overcome the Hidden Struggles of Living with ADHD. Embrace Neurodiversity and Learn the Best Emotional Control Strategies Thanks to the Power of Self-Discipline

MARY JANE GOALS

Introduction

The term ADHD came into existence in the early 1980s and is still not officially recognized by the APA (American Psychiatric Association) or the World Health Organization but is widely used worldwide. The terms ADD/ADHD are often used interchangeably with ADHD, but there are subtle differences.

ADHD is an abbreviation for attention-deficit /hyperactivity disorder. It's a brain disorder characterized by restlessness, impulsiveness, and difficulty concentrating on tasks that require sustained focus.

There is no known answer to when and where this disorder started. The condition appears to have been created quite early in human history. There are many different theories on how this disorder came into being. One of them is that ADHD was a mixture of other mental illnesses that may have been combined over time.

There is also the chance that men were simply the first to develop ADHD. They were exposed to high levels of dopamine at an earlier age than women because they are significantly more physically active than women as a whole.

There are many theories and misconceptions about adult ADHD. Not much is known about ADHD in women, but it is still an important topic. Women with ADHD often find themselves struggling more than men because of how society perceives them, their different symptoms, and the treatments available for them. Adult women with ADHD can find themselves feeling isolated, unsupported, or frustrated by the disorder.

The exact cause of ADHD is not clear, and it may be that there are several reasons for the symptoms. Similarly, exposure to drugs, alcohol, or other chemicals during pregnancy may cause ADHD in the mother. While these environmental factors are possible causes, research suggests that different brain areas appear to be affected by the disorder.

Studies have shown that women with ADHD have more trouble with planning and organization, another symptom of the disorder. Studies have shown that 60 percent of untreated ADHD in adults is due to depression, anxiety, or a chemical imbalance in the brain.

This book talks about the different symptoms of ADHD in women. It also talks about how society perceives them and the various treatments available for them. ADHD impacts women more than men because societal norms are not as accepting of their types of symptoms. If you are feeling isolated, unsupported, or frustrated because of this disorder, this book will open you up to strategies that will help you get better.

If you are an executive or have a high-stress job, you may have to concentrate very hard on the tasks at hand and may have trouble shifting your focus away from work when you go home. As a result, chores around the house often get neglected until it's too late, and you find yourself drowning in dirty dishes and laundry.

Women with ADHD tend to be more sensitive to stress than men and have consistent difficulty managing their emotions. Women with ADHD also commonly have problems with time management, adapting to change, and following instructions. In addition to these symptoms, some women report that they feel numb towards life. Other's report feeling emotionally abandoned by loved ones when their ADHD was not recognized or appropriately managed.

Generally, this book is suitable for both men and women. However, the central focus is on women who are more prone to this disorder. I would recommend that women with ADHD read this book, as it may provide some helpful insights into the condition and how to deal with negative emotions.

Meditation for ADHD (Positivity and Encouragement)

Do you have ADHD? Do you want to learn how to use meditation for ADHD women with joy and without the negativity which often accompanies the topic? You are in luck!

Since I have been diagnosed with ADHD, I have had a lot of trouble figuring out how to deal with it.

I found my way through meditation. It has helped my brain stay calm and clear. It also helps me keep focused on what is important (and not worry about everything else around me).

I have learned that ADHD is not an illness. It is a neurobiological difference which can (and should) be treated.

Meditation focuses on the positive and helps you maintain a positive attitude in stressful situations. It also helps you keep your brain on track and not constantly distracted by thoughts which do not matter to you.

This is why I want to teach others about meditation for ADHD women.

I have started the organization, A Noble Dream, to help those who suffer from ADHD and other mental illnesses.

My organization will help people find a way to keep their brains focused and clear while helping them avoid drugs which may not be right for them.

So far, I have only mentioned meditation as my method of therapy.

Why? Because it is the method I have chosen, and it works.

I know many people have a hard time learning how to meditate and the reasons vary.

For ADHD women, meditation can be difficult because of our high activity levels (which is why medication was often necessary).

Our minds are constantly racing, and we get distracted easily. This can make it seem impossible to keep our focus on one thing and not jump from one thing to another.

In my opinion, though, all we need to do is to follow a mantra.

We can all use a mantra.

"I am focused."

"I am alert."

"I am calm."

This is what I have been telling myself for many years and it has helped me greatly.

So, if you suffer from ADHD and you want to learn how to use meditation as therapy, then this article will help get you started on your journey.

First things first.

You need to find a way to meditate which is comfortable for you. If you want to be successful with meditation, then you should try different ways of doing it and see which one helps you the most.

Meditation can be done in many different fashions and in many different locations:

- At home (or any other place you want)
- A quiet room with no lights or distractions.
- At your office or at school (after hours).
- At your favorite yoga classes.
- At a special class where they have certain lights or music geared towards you.
- In a special room with just the right noise level and lighting.

If you are new to meditation, I suggest learning how to meditate in these different locations so that you can find which works best for you.

I also recommend using the internet to learn about different meditation methods and see which one's work for you. You can search for websites about meditation or YouTube channels pertaining to this subject. You will find that not only do the videos which are free save your money, but they also offer different ways of studying and learning how to meditate.

As I said earlier, I have found that meditation helps keep my mind clear and focused.

In fact, most days I am able to sit down for 20-40 minutes without needing any help (sometimes even longer).

I have also learned that I should sit in one spot and not move.

This is because moving will break my concentration and I will have to start over.

I learned that moving around with ADHD is not a good idea, even if you feel like it will help you stay focused. This goes against everything you may have experienced in your life and your brain takes time to adjust to the ways of meditation.

The goal of meditation is to learn how to keep your mind clear and focused on one thing at one time (without needing outside assistance).

Meditation is a tool for dealing with stress and anxiety. It's also an effective tool for improving focus, attention, happiness, and self-esteem. For children with ADHD (attention deficit hyperactivity disorder) meditation has been shown to have significant benefits that are often sustained long term.

Meditation can be used in conjunction with other interventions such as therapy or medication to help improve the ADHD symptoms of executive function deficits and sleep problems. . ..

Although there are many methods of meditation, it is useful to have clear objectives, a time frame and a teacher to guide you. One method of meditation which is often used with children with ADHD is called "Mindfulness." Mindfulness which is also referred to as "Focused Attention" teaches the person to become aware of their mind and body. The practice starts from the simple act of being aware that you are breathing in and out.

One of the advantages of this practice is that it is easy to understand and can be taught to very young children. The main idea of mindfulness is being able to focus attention on one specific thing for a reasonable period of time, whether it be your breath, someone else's words or any other thing.

One method in teaching children how to meditate on their breath involves simply having them lie down on the floor and listen to one person. With their eyes closed they breathe in and out. This type of practice is usually carried out by parents and can be set up as a regular routine. However, the benefits come from reflecting on the process and being aware at all times that you are breathing in and out.

The benefits of mindfulness don't only come from being aware of your own breaths. Other methods such as forgiveness meditation encourages children to be kind to themselves. For example, there are many different ways teachers have used "Kindness Meditation" with their students at school or home.

A simple and clear meditation for ADHD.

This meditation helps you overcome the emotional challenges of living with ADHD, depression, or anxiety and is useful for any time of the day.

It consists of a visualization exercise that focuses on your natural radiance and connection to positivity. It uses cognitive behavioral therapy techniques as it teaches you to focus your attention towards the benefits that life offers rather than the difficulties it brings.

It is also very helpful for runners as it can be used before or during a run as a method of relaxation and focus.

 It is also extremely useful for athletes of any kind since it unleashes your natural energy and allows you to reach your highest potential.

Meditation is a way to relax and let go of the difficulties in your life. It's recommended for people who have difficulty focusing and feeling calm. Meditation also helps reduce stress in the body and mind with better health, mood, focus, happiness, creativity, productivity and motivation.

Women With ADHD

Why girls and women are under-diagnosed

Although ADHD is typically only seen in children, it can also affect women of all ages and has negative impacts on the quality of life. The symptoms may not be as obvious in females, causing them to be under-diagnosed and therefore under-treated. They may experience some but not all ADHD symptoms, or they may display symptoms differently than males. Symptoms that are less common in females include:

Some studies suggest that women with ADHD tend to have an earlier age of onset (though this is not always the case). Females are also exposed to higher levels of estrogen throughout their lifetimes, this change in estrogen levels may lead to a disruption in the development of executive functioning skills. Executive functioning skills are critical for planning, organization and self-awareness.

Additionally, women with ADHD have higher rates of co-morbid disorders including depression (6x more likely), anxiety (10x more likely), eating disorders (8x more likely), alcohol abuse (2.9x more likely). and drug abuse (2.9x more likely.)

Because ADHD is complex and often under recognized in women, it can have a negative impact on their quality of life throughout all stages of adulthood. Many ADHD patients are successful in childhood and even adolescence, but this does not always hold true for adults. This is compared to 53% of those without diagnosed ADHD symptoms. Without proper treatment many women are unable to complete college or obtain high-paying jobs. Studies suggest that the number of females per available jobs is higher than males by 22%. Also, females with ADHD tend to earn less than their male counterparts.

Even emotional and physical well-being is impacted. A study published in 2010 found that women with ADHD were more than twice as likely to have a car accident. Additionally, they are 63% more likely to report having eating disorders and 71% more likely to have a clinically significant level of depression in their lifetime.

ADHD is also linked with noncompliance. In a study of adult patients who were diagnosed, 89% of participants had trouble taking medications as prescribed due to the fact that they could not remember or follow through on the plan as given to them by their doctor.

In addition to the possible links between ADHD and accidents, females with ADHD are also more likely to smoke cigarettes, drink alcohol excessively and use illicit drugs.

ADHD is a complex disorder that can manifest in different ways in women than males. As a result, symptoms are often not as obvious as in males, leading to under-diagnosis and therefore under-treatment. Women may experience some but not all of the symptoms of ADHD, or their symptoms may be different from those seen in males. There is a higher risk for females to have other disorders at the same time or at least higher rates of comorbidity. The risk of ADHD is one of the highest for a psychiatric disorder with the highest percentage of comorbid disorders being depression and anxiety disorders. Lack of emotional connection is common in females with ADHD, which can lead to poor treatment compliance.

The symptoms that are most common in women include:

ADHD medications may be effective for women without other conditions or those who do not have co-morbidities. However, treatment is not as effective for those with at least one other condition therefore further research is needed into how these patients can be treated and managed. This is important because ADHD in women is often under-diagnosed and poorly treated. This leads to many of the negative social, emotional, cognitive and behavioral problems seen in women with this disorder.

There are three major types of drugs that are used for ADHD treatment:

For females who do not have other conditions or co-morbidities, the recommended treatment is typically psychostimulants. A meta-analysis of 13 studies shows that psychostimulants were found to be effective for treating ADHD symptoms in both males and females. However, one study suggests that females respond to methylphenidate as well as males.

For females who have co-morbid conditions (e.g. depression, anxiety or eating disorders) or comorbidity with these conditions, the recommended treatment is usually a combination of psychostimulants and non-stimulants. A study on methylphenidate in females in particular showed that these women respond to the same dose as males. However, there are less studies for those with comorbid conditions and therefore more research is necessary to determine their effectiveness.

In order to increase the number of women with ADHD who are able to obtain treatment, it is important that they are correctly identified and diagnosed. Male and female symptoms of ADHD can be different, and only an accurate diagnosis can lead to effective treatment. Women may also be less likely than men to seek help for their problems, either due to low self-esteem or denial that their symptoms are related to a disorder. Sex role stereotypes can also impact whether or not females acknowledge they have ADHD, as they worry about the idea of having less control and being viewed as irresponsible.

While females have been diagnosed with ADHD at similar rates to males in the past, the diagnosis for women has recently declined. This may be due to a variety of reasons including:

Once females are diagnosed with ADHD, it is important that they get appropriate treatment if they wish to improve their lives. According to an unpublished study performed by Richard Milich (a psychologist, teacher and researcher), one-third of female students at a large Southeastern university scored above cutoff on the ASRS-v1.1 (the diagnostic instrument he developed for adults) while only one-half of them indicated that they had been ever treated for ADHD despite many having life impairing symptoms.

If a woman has been diagnosed with ADHD and is seeking treatment, there are various options available to her. Medications can be prescribed in order to help with the symptoms of ADHD. It is recommended that women take medication under the supervision of their doctors. These therapy options include psychoeducation, cognitive behavioral therapy, drug therapy and ADHD coaching, among others. A combination approach is often recommended because it helps with long-term outcomes as opposed to just addressing one issue at a time.

Struggles of Women with ADHD

If you have ADHD, you're no different from anyone else. You might be able to multitask better than most people and have a refreshing perspective on life. No matter what your struggle is, there's something about ADHD that makes you who you are.

It makes it hard for you to concentrate for long periods of time. Also, it makes it hard to control impulsive behavior. This means that you have trouble controlling your emotions, and you might get annoyed easily. It's also hard to sit still or pay attention for very long. All in all, ADHD makes it really hard to focus on one thing and finish a lot of tasks.

Besides having symptoms like these, ADHD can also cause many other problems like high stress levels and sleeping problems. It's hard to handle all of this, but you are not alone. Most people with ADHD also feel very stressed about it, but there are ways to make your life easier.

Inattentive is when people don't pay attention and have a hard time focusing on anything for very long, and hyperactive-impulsive is when they're impulsive and have trouble controlling their movements or feelings.

It's hard to believe sometimes that people with ADHD can also be very smart. They might be really good at some things like programming, math, or sports. Most people with ADHD have very good memory skills, and they can think about things very quickly. You might know someone who has ADHD and they're very bright and enthusiastic.

There are also many strengths that come with having ADHD too. Many people with ADHD have a refreshing perspective on life; they live every day to the fullest and usually take every new situation as a gift. They are energetic, flexible, and active, a little bit like the energizer bunny in women's books. Many of them like sports or being around other people. They're usually very social and like to be around other people, or they do things that are fun and exciting. You might know someone who is very energetic or is always up for an adventure.

You also might know someone who is very artistic, creative, or has a good imagination. They can complement others and have a good sense of humor. They might also have great intuition and become aware of situations before they happen. They can be great leaders too because they're motivated to help others get to where they want to go.

Of course, there are also some struggles with having ADHD too. Having ADHD means that you have to work really hard to control your behavior and pay attention in school. You might also have a hard time at home doing things around the house or paying attention when your mother is talking.

But there's nothing wrong with having ADHD. It's just like any other disorder or disability; it just makes it harder for you to focus on things. You can still be an amazing athlete or artist and do everything you want to do in life if you have the right help. "It can be very frustrating for people with ADHD, but they learn ways to cope and manage their condition." (Leahy)They become smarter by figuring out how they learn best and how they can handle their problems. They become stronger by knowing how to advocate for themselves and asking for help when they need it. They can be great leaders because they know what it's like to struggle and how to keep going.

Having ADHD doesn't mean that you're inferior. It just means that you have to learn a different way of doing things, and you might need some extra help along the way. But just like anyone else, you can be just as successful in life no matter what your strengths or struggles are.

Psychological and Emotional Effects of ADHD on women

ADHD or Attention Deficit Hyperactivity Disorder is a disorder that can impact the lives of both male and female sufferers. This article will focus on the emotional and psychological effects ADHD has on women as opposed to men. Women are very sensitive emotionally and have different emotions than men. They feel things more deeply, worry about things for longer periods of time, take action when they see something good happen, etcetera. These reasons make them more likely to be affected by ADHD.

Females are more likely to get diagnosed with ADHD, but males can also suffer from the disorder. Girls are not usually diagnosed with ADHD until they are in elementary school or high school; however, boys are often diagnosed in elementary school or early grades of middle school. Boys have problems getting their teacher's attention, focusing on tasks, organized and productive behavior and maintaining behavioral control. Females can suffer from these same symptoms, but they may gravitate towards different emotions as well. Females will most likely feel like there is no reason or purpose for what they are doing. They show increased grief, sadness, lower self-confidence, guilt, shame and low self-worth on top of the symptoms that males have. ADHD can lead to many problems in a girl's life including trouble in school, at work or with friends. The severity of the disorder will also dictate how many problems a girl will have. Women and girls are much more likely to have academic problems than males, and this is the most common sign of ADHD in females. Females that have ADHD have trouble with time management, they forget things when they do them or do them at the last minute and they have problems following through with projects. Females with ADHD often feel like other students are out to get them, due to jealousy. They also have feelings of being unloved, isolated, rebellious and victimized. Teens with ADHD are more likely to be rejected by their peers as a result of their ADHD. When they are young they are teased and when they enter the teen years they become isolated. As women grow older they continue to have problems with maintaining close relationships, they can't remember things that are told to them and they may forget appointments and everyday necessities. Many suffer from depression as a result of this disorder.

It is important for females with ADHD to seek treatment for their emotional and psychological issues as it is an issue that can get worse without treatment. Females that are young need to be given a good education so that they can learn how to manage their behavior. They will also have problems in school such as dropping out, failing tests, forgetting homework, etcetera. As they grow older they will continue to suffer from academic difficulties due to failure or poor grades caused by ADHD. Women with ADHD need to be given treatment because they need to know how to manage their behavior so they can get through life and maintain their relationships. They need to know how to properly control themselves that they will not get in trouble with the law or face major penalties socially. They need to learn how to follow through on their chores and also understand when to back off from a task. Women with ADHD will suffer from emotional issues such as loneliness, lack of confidence, low self-esteem and believing others are against them. They will often feel depressed and even develop eating disorders along with the other effects ADHD can have on a person.

Morale Managing

Morale Managing & Leadership Coaching has been designed with women in mind. The following article will show you how to manage and lead a team of women with ADHD.

They are women, in fact there are many women in the workforce, and they are all over the world. The most popular careers among women include education, media, fashion retailing and others such as hospitality service industry.

Women with ADHD need to be objective when it comes to their job performance because they have many conflicting ideas between them and require clear direction from management. Women with ADHD are very sensitive and need constant supervision, feedback and respect. They are hyperactive and vigorous, but they will slow right down once they know the direction in which they want to go. Women with ADHD are usually independent thinkers who need to be redirected by an authority figure who is ready to help them in a variety of ways, such as; understanding that their workloads need to be adjusted on a regular basis, or reminded why they chose their career path in the first place.

Having a strong group of women with ADHD can be difficult, but it is easy when you know how to manage their attention and organize them around a common goal.

Women with ADHD are multitaskers and this is one reason why they need clear leadership and management in place. They are ready to work hard for the company, but they also want to be productive by getting the job done faster.

If you are a manager, this is what you need to know.

Women with ADHD can be found in any type of workplace. In fact, the very first female astronaut was born with ADHD. On top of that, in reaction to women's roles in the workforce, many companies have included their becoming part-time mothers as a priority.

How do you manage them?

Manage them as much as possible by giving them clear priorities and accountability for every task.

Women with ADHD naturally love to work, but they also need to feel productive. You know that feeling when you get a lot done in a short time and are ready for something new? Women with ADHD have that persevering quality.

You must seize the opportunity to manage them. Do the following:

Set clear goals and deadlines for your women's projects, if they get their tasks completed early you will be rewarded. If they are behind schedule, it means more stress on them and their productivity will suffer.

People with ADHD work best in small teams. This way, you will be able to assign them tasks according to what they specialize in. As a manager, you need to know that women with ADHD can easily be replaced by other staff members. You cannot do everything yourself.

When assigning projects, I always look for the best possible combination of ideas and participation of everyone on the team. In fact, a project should never have just one person in charge of it, but rather each team member should bring something unique to the table. If that person cannot complete the project, then you should think about picking a different one.

Give women with ADHD the staff badly needed breaks. They tend to work too much and they become irritable if they are not given a chance to take their mind off of things. This is why it is important to have an opportunity to take a break often, whether that means shutting down your computer for 10 minutes or having a quick walk in nature with your coworkers.

Remember, everyone has a different style when it comes to work. Some people are more direct and decisive and others are more laid back and friendly.

How do you find the best fit for your organization? I recommend that you think about including a woman on your employee database that would be priority for you to hire.

For example, by considering women with ADHD as a section of your workforce you will have a number of very diverse points of view, which is a good thing when it comes down to making decisions that affect the workplace.

You can also ask your friends and coworkers what they think about women with ADHD in the workforce, which will give you great feedback.

Practical Tips and Exercises to Improve Your Memory and Attention Span

Memory is a superpower, and almost everyone has potential to be better. A little bit of effort at the right time can make a big difference in your daily life. Take control of your memory today with these practical tips and exercises!

The Right Way to Learn Memory Exercises

. It is also important to understand how you can use them most effectively. An effective cognitive technique is a fairly simple one: three steps that last for 30 minutes, three times a week. And whenever you skip your memory exercises, you will find the results harder to achieve in the future.

In this article, I want to propose some useful tips that will make it easier for you to remember your upcoming goals. And I will also present some of the best memory exercises you can use, based on psychology and neuroscience.

Visualization as a Memory Exercise

Visualization is a powerful technique that anyone can use. It is one of the most effective ways to prepare for something, especially when it comes to sports, exams and speeches. Visualization helps you to "practice" or rehearse your upcoming event, while your brain creates mental images of the actual thing.

The most common approach is to visualize yourself arriving on time, behaving naturally and walking up to the stage without difficulty.

This technique helps you to feel confident and prepared, but it also has a functional purpose. When you imagine yourself doing something, your brain creates new synaptic connections between neurons that help you preview the real situation.

Memory is a superpower, and almost everyone has potential to be better. A little bit of effort at the right time can make a big difference in your daily life. Take control of your memory today with these practical tips and exercises!

Mind clearing is a very important part of improving your memory. By clearing your mind, you will be able to focus more and improve your concentration. In this article, we listed the most common methods for improving your mind-clearing skills and many other applications for them.

The first step in improving your memory is to find a way to memorize things better. This might include different ways of learning from repetition, visual tricks and different forms of concentration. Learning these different techniques and creating a schedule for yourself can help you better remember things for an extended period of time.

If you are looking to memorize something by repetition, you want to make sure it's properly stored in your brain. To do this, you must be able to utilize both the right and left side of your brain simultaneously. Use repetition with a visualization technique when trying to commit something to memory.

One common method that people use to memorize is the method of loci, or memory palaces. This is a system of visualizing different places in your mind. These could be anything from the control room of a starship to a garden shed to your house.

Something that is often used by scientists and doctors to memorize things is mnemonics, which are sequences of words, phrases or numbers that aid memory recall. There are many different techniques for memorizing things through mnemonics: you can use concrete associations to the words, use figurative language or create rhyming phrases.

Another technique to improve your memory is to take advantage of colors and geometry. Using colors can help you memorize better and faster, while a good understanding of geometry will help you arrange and organize things better.

65% of adults over the age of 20 have forgotten their Social Security number! This is one way to prevent yourself from forgetting important information. If you don't want to forget your Social

Security number, write it down and carry it around with you so that you can reference it whenever possible.

How to Improve Stress Management and Impulsive Behavior to Be More Efficient in Every Situation and Lead a Fulfilling Life

The right decisions for dealing with stress and impulse issues can have a direct effect on whether you sleep well, maintain a healthy weight, stay in love, or find peace of mind.

Impulse and stressful situations are an everyday occurrence for you, but there's no need to lose your cool, fight back, or run away every time a crisis hit.

Here are some tips to help you:

1 – Take care of yourself first.

The first step is to take care of yourself so that you can deal with the demands of life more effectively. You need to find the strength from within in order to improve how you manage stress, stay organized and sustain your energy levels throughout the day.

These daily habits will improve your ability to manage stress and impulse control.

Good sleep habits: Having a good night's sleep can help you calm down, overcome negative emotions and take the right decisions. Most people with ADHD have a sleep disorder which can cause insomnia, restless legs syndrome, night sweats, etc. See an expert if you are having difficulty with sleeping.

Eat everyday: Eating five to six small meals a day instead of three big ones will increase your energy levels.

Exercise: Regular exercise can not only improve mood but also help you maintain a healthy weight.

Meditate: Meditation can bring peace of mind, enhance motivation and improve sleep. See an expert if you are seeking activities or ways to relieve stress and anxiety.

Get organized: Keeping your home, car and workspace organized will help you become more efficient.

2 – Practice mindfulness.

It can increase your ability to handle stress in a positive way because it helps you recognize how best to deal with problematic feelings, so you don't react out of anger or aggression; but instead take a more positive approach.

Mindfulness is also a way to focus your attention on the present moment, bringing you into a state of awareness and allowing you to respond rather than react impulsively.

3 – Get support.

Supporting others will improve your stress management. You can nurture new friendships and have fun through activities that bring peace of mind, such as meditation or yoga classes.

4 – Delegate.

Get support from others by delegating tasks to family members and friends. Delegating tasks is a great way to relieve the stress of everyday life and lets you have time for yourself. But you need to be kind and not push too much. Let others do their share so your stress levels don't get out of hand.

5 – Have realistic expectations and reminders.

When you have realistic expectations, it will be easier to stay focused on what's real, because the real goal is to improve quality of life and the capacity to manage stress and keep your energy up.

6 – Not everyone lives and functions the same.

Not everyone's life works with the same priorities or has the same demands; some people are more organized than others. And some people are just better at managing stress. But there is no need to feel inferior, because although everyone's situation may be different, you can always improve yourself so you can function more effectively.

"Mindfulness" Meditation For ADHD: Learn How to Practice This Activity, Proven Effective in Improving Concentration and Promoting Relaxation of The Body and Mind

Women who have ADHD face stressful events and pressures. Meditation, with or without ADHD drugs, should be part of the management regimen that increases the quality of life. According to research, meditation may help reduce destructive ADHD-related symptoms, including difficulty concentrating and impulsivity.

Women with ADHD have traditionally been an underserved category and pay a high price as a result. A delayed diagnosis, a misdiagnosis, and a lack of real ADHD knowledge translate to years of unnecessary struggle, poor self-esteem, being marginalized, and thinking something is flawed with them. As a result, women with ADHD can benefit greatly from mindfulness. Some women can go their entire life without ever realizing they have ADHD. This can be a very upsetting feeling for many women, who all too frequently find themselves in the unfortunate situation of "moving on" without assistance when an adequate diagnosis could greatly change their lives. Furthermore, those who seek treatment with possible signs run the risk of being misdiagnosed with another illness, such as mood disturbance or anxiety. The result, though, remains the same: a lack of assistance and care for the appropriate conditions, which could contribute to more mental health issues. Women with ADHD often experience profound tension as they try to maintain an outwardly natural character that satisfies social demands and desires while simultaneously coping with an influx of ADHD symptoms frequently compounded by changing hormones over time. This dynamic can also contribute to burnouts daily. Females with ADHD sometimes conceal how much time it takes to get through each day, secretly wondering how other women seem to have it so simple. Meanwhile, their stray thoughts, interests, and sacrifices are overlooked in a society that struggles to accommodate minds that think differently. It is not shocking that living this way can lead to increased anxiety, feelings of inferiority, and deterioration of self-esteem over time. It is difficult to be accused of being dreamy or careless when you are trying nonstop to keep life going, feeling bad when it fails, and drained when it is complete. Overall, the feeling can be debilitating, leaving those who are masking ADHD in desperate need of help.

Meditation may not be the only means of treating your ADHD, but it can help to ease the symptoms. There are many forms of meditation, which means that there is one that works better on your brain. Personalized mantras, for example, can be especially powerful due to their familiarity. Mantra meditation, as opposed to deliberately focusing on silencing a busy or disturbed mind, asks you to repeat a sentence in your head and let it take you naturally to a place of peace and rest. So, consider the right methods of meditations if you are a woman with ADHD because not all forms work. Mantra meditation has the virtue of providing little space for the mind to drift. This is one of the most difficult obstacles for beginners of meditations and women with ADHD and those who suffer the most with concentration. This refocusing of the mind, if performed daily, will help clear your mind and strengthen your concentration.

Meditation, in addition to its relaxing and de-stressing properties, can help develop communication abilities over time by promoting pauses and contemplation. Women with better communication skills are less likely to be stressed in meetings and social settings and can strike a happy medium while communicating with others. This can help women with ADHD control their impulsivity, letting them have better communication in their daily lives, which in turn will alleviate stress during usually uncomfortable situations.

Meditation allows your brain and body to reach a deeper resting state than even your longest sleep. Tapping into this state allows the prefrontal cortex to fully relax. As a result, cortisol and other stress chemicals are decreased by up to a quarter, while happy hormone output increases, leaving you even more resistant to unwanted yet unavoidable future stress. This is vital for women with ADHD because it alleviates stress and paranoia while also building morale and encouraging them to be more loyal to themselves. Meditation can be performed whenever and wherever the individual requires it, making it the ideal, independent method for ADHD symptom control. Although meditation is not a substitute for ADHD treatment, it can be used as part of a holistic recovery strategy to greatly contribute to the betterment of women with ADHD. Mindfulness and meditation enable you to devote attention to your emotions and emotional wellbeing so that you do not behave recklessly and respond differently to tense situations.

After a lifetime of rushing emotions, it can be difficult to picture yourself happily seated in the lotus pose. You do not have to sit or even quit moving to meditate, which is a little-known secret. You can meditate using music. It does not need to be in silence. You can use melody to practice your breathing patterns. It is acceptable to have your thoughts drift away from meditation. Try to disengage and move your focus back to meditation. You can find yourself doing this multiple times at first, and that is fine. Understand that meditation is something that requires practice, and there is no right or wrong in this. Do this activity not to judge yourself but to better your state of mind. When you meditate, calm your agitated body with quick, repeated motions such as walking. Start by meditating for a few minutes a day and increase the time as it becomes more manageable. Try to stick to it and make this a habit. If you find it hard to stick to this as a routine, try enrolling in a meditation course or organize regular meetups with a close friend. You can make use of mobile applications as well. Meditation can help you deal with difficult feelings at work or home. It helps you to take a step back from the chaos and concentrate on your relevant field. You can keep seeing both optimistic and bad interactions. However, if you learn to relax and control your tension, you and those around you can enjoy the happiness you deserve. Throw out your preconceived notions of meditation because you do not have to sit silently to do it. Most meditation applications are online. Download a lot, then pick your favorite. Perhaps a certain narrator's voice irritates you, or another's tone appeals to you more than the others. Each application begins with a step-by-step explanation of how to be conscious. Breathing seems to be easy, doesn't it? Breathing is the first ability you must learn before you can meditate to control your concentration and feelings, which might sound strange. You start by counting to five as you breathe in and counting to seven as you breathe out. There is no magic number; just take as many breaths as you feel comfortable. It is difficult to plan your time while you have ADHD. Finding time for yourself is much more difficult. Some hardly have time to take a shower, let alone meditate for a half-hour a day. When you first start to meditate, you can notice that your response to physical stress changes. You no longer get a feeling of overwhelm, and if you do, it can be much easier to get rid of that feeling. Prioritizing can get easier with the help of meditation too. It can feel easier to decide which tasks need to be tackled first. Once you master meditation, you should be able to function better at home and work. You should stop striving to be perfect and believe you are the best version of yourself. Meditation can help you hinder your negative self-talk and change the way you think and look at yourself. According to research, cognitive meditation for ADHD will teach the brain to properly concentrate and maintain focus. Keeping focus and managing to self-regulate are two persistent regular obstacles for both adults and children with ADHD. As a normal ADHD treatment, it stands to reason that any kind of concentration training that also improves self-control will be invaluable and extremely effective.

Mindful meditation, also known as mindfulness, is used in various religious cultures. Buddhism, for example, includes a form of mindful practice known as vipassana. If you are not spiritual or religious, it does not mean you cannot meditate. It entails paying careful attention to your emotions, feelings, and physiological sensations; in other words, having a better sense of what is going on with you at any given time. It can be used to promote health, especially psychological well-being. ADHD medication cannot work on inner skills, unlike meditation. It helps to increase your capacity to self-observe, train attention, and build new relationships to stressful experiences, strengthening your ability to monitor your attention. In other words, it helps you to give heed to paying attention, and it will also make people more mindful of their psychological response, preventing them from reacting recklessly. For a long time, researchers have discussed using meditation to treat ADHD, but the challenge has always been whether people with ADHD can use it, particularly if they are overactive. Mindfulness's adaptability and simplicity allow for individuality in the strategy, allowing it to fit for you. The trick is to practice mindfulness during your day, constantly being conscious of where your concentration is directed when doing repetitive tasks. For instance, you might find that your mind wanders when driving. Many people exercise mindfulness as they snack. Once you are used to tuning in with yourself and your body, you can use the practice whenever you're feeling stressed.

How To Prevent Attention Deficit Hyperactivity Disorder from Affecting Your Relationships, So You Can Have Healthy, Happy Relationships with Everyone You Love

Attention Deficit Hyperactivity Disorder (ADHD) is a neurological disorder that affects up to 10% of children and adults. It is one of the most common psychiatric diagnoses in children, yet only 20-25% receive treatment. There are different types and levels of ADHD that can manifest itself in different ways, and for some it doesn't look like ADHD at all.

This article will teach you how to identify ADHD behaviors, what their origins could be, and what steps you can take to make sure your relationships stay healthy.

Dealing with ADHD can be a difficult task. ADHD sufferers are often misunderstood not only by their family and friends but society itself.

ADD/ADHD is categorized as a mental disorder, but it's more than just being lazy or spacing out. It's a neurological condition marked by poor concentration, impulsivity, and hyperactivity that interferes with functioning or development.

In fact, many with the disorder move around so frequently and are in such constant motion that they may seem like they are driven by a motor.

Now this may or may not be you, but if you find yourself thinking or writing down that you have ADHD, one thing to do is look at how your brain functions and what triggers it.

How to identify ADHD behavior?

ADHD has three main symptoms that are consistent throughout an individual's life. These are:

Impulsivity: The person may act on impulse and not think before they act. They often jump from one activity to another with little or no thought of what is in between or if there is even a purpose for doing the activities in the first place.

Hyperactivity: This can be difficulty sitting still, constant motion, inability to remain seated at times.

Inattention: The person may have difficulty paying attention to the information being given or may show lack of focus.

How to treat ADHD behavior?

1. Identify what triggers the behavior. Your family, friends and even doctors may not be able to identify what causes your ADHD habits as these behaviors can be caused by many factors outside of genetics or brain structure, including stress and sleep deprivation. Perhaps your medication is interfering with your brain function.

2. Learn to control your thoughts and feelings. Medication, diet and exercise are some of the ways you can control your thoughts and feelings that may cause you to behave in odd ways.

3. Have a plan for when life gets too busy and stressful. Have a plan for coping with the daily stresses and do what it takes to stay on top of things you need to do.

4. Deal with the stress in a healthy way. Stress is bad for anybody, but it can cause you to act out in ways that are against your better judgment and will teach you that some behaviors are not acceptable.

5. Remember that ADHD is manageable and can be controlled. You can control what you do, especially in your daily life. The solutions are in your hands, so try to recognize how you can change how you act and deal with situations in a different way.

6. Think of people with the same issues as you and learn how they handle stress better than you do. People with ADHD are often singled out for criticism because their actions do not seem like they "should.

7. Get in touch with people who have ADHD and ask them how they deal with their condition. You may be surprised by what you find out.

8. Identify stressors that don't affect you but affect others around you and learn to deal with them effectively. For example, if your spouse is always stressed, don't let it interfere with your own life or make things tense at home. Take time to talk about the problems and come up with a solution together instead of letting it ruin your marriage over something so small.

9.	Learn to say NO. If you can, don't feel obligated to do certain things or take on things that may not benefit you in the long run. Know how to say No and WHY you are saying No.
10.	Learn how to be assertive, not aggressive when you want someone to do something for you and make them feel accountable for making a decision that affects other people around them.

Tips That Will Help You Be More Organized in Your Life, Not Forgetting Anything and Allowing You to Achieve Any Goal

Many adult women can struggle with clutter in both the home and the workplace, leaving them feeling exhausted or trapped. Getting coordinated will benefit you in various ways, including increasing efficiency, reducing fear, giving up time wasted searching for stuff, and serving as a good role model for your children

Getting tasks underway is one of the most difficult aspects of making a transition. Reward systems or promotions will assist you in being more prepared. Until you begin an organizational project, decide on a prize for yourself after you've completed it. When you've finished the job, make sure to reward yourself. Having a friend assist you will make the job simpler and quicker, especially if you need to declutter. Friends will assist you with getting rid of items because they do not have the same emotional connection to them as you do. You may also find social help in online chat communities. Some have features where you make clear promises to arrange a room, then leave your computer to organize for a while before returning to support each other. You may benefit from using a timer or music. The timer can be programmed to go off in 15-minute intervals, with 15-minute breaks in between. Breaking down a difficult task into simpler steps and tackling these steps one at a time is the only way to master it.

Try the following steps to organize a physical space:

1. Choose the spaces to be organized. Make a list of the areas you want to declutter.

2. Arrange them in descending order of difficulty. You may write these down on post-its and stick them to your refrigerator or on the notice board in your study. Estimate how long each task can take you to complete. Once you establish how long it can take you, try dividing that time into smaller intervals with short breaks in between. Do not pretend to clear a whole room in 3 hours without having a break. You can be headed for failure if you do. Dividing the task into realistic intervals can get you a higher rate of success, and as you might have figured by now, starting is a big hurdle for people with ADHD. Once you start off performing the task, you feel a sense of accomplishment which convinces you to persevere and complete it as planned.

3. Begin with the simplest space. Starting easy can maximize your chances of completing the task and being successful. Because people with ADHD feed off adrenaline rush and stimulation, succeeding at one task can make you more likely to complete the following ones. Divide the room into parts and focus on one at a time, arranging, discarding, or reorganizing each item in that section until it is completed. Dividing the space, you want to organize into quarters can be very helpful. You can plan to declutter a quarter of the room in 30 minutes, for example. This can give you a more realistic notion of time and its management. People with ADHD can struggle with this attribute because they have a false sense of time. When organizing your room, try to keep things according to their function. Keep things where you know you use them and can find them later. If you need cleaning supplies or other things to organize your space, make sure to prepare it before starting on the task. If you need garbage bags or vacuum cleaners, make sure you have them available; otherwise, it can be very easy to get

distracted. When clearing your space, decide whether you can get rid of some things, box them, store them away, or keep them handy.

4. Choose an incentive or inspiration to promote the completion of this task. Once you complete the task, make sure you reward yourself.

5. When the smallest room is arranged, work your way up to the most complex, repeating steps if necessary.

6. Another challenge can be staying organized and maintaining the hard work you have just done. If you work with paper, recycle or trash unnecessary ones. If you can, try working electronically and limit the paper piles. Try using a scanner or an application on your phone to save soft copies of important documents. Create a filing system. Make sure you file every day if possible or as frequently as required to avoid cluttering your space again.

7. You can create storage space if your area is limited. If you work from your room, try storing work material under your bed or use over-the-door organizers to store smaller things like stationery and pantry items. These would usually hang on the side of a cabinet or a door and helps to create storage space. They are usually made either of fabric or plastic and can be bought from your local store for cheap. Besides creating storage space, they also organize your space and help you put things in one spot. Store things where you are likely to spot them easily when needed. This can save you time and frustration.

Try these tips for staying organized and limit the clutter:

- If whilst you clean, you end up discovering long-lost items and do not know where they go, collect them in a box and after you are done cleaning, try finding them adequate space.

- Work at the moment by putting things away immediately when you realize they are out of order. If you walk by an open drawer, close it. If your waste in is full, empty it. If you see clothes lying around on the floor, pick them up and put them in the laundry basket straight away. If you notice some papers lying around, file them.

- Take ten minutes from your day to clean up around the house. This small step every day can alleviate the burden of having to devote bigger chunks of your day just to clean up your space.
- The most difficult part is getting started, but once you start and see that you are making gains, you are more inclined to stick with it. Try to adopt a mindset that allows you to believe you will only stick to this task for a stipulated amount of time. Once you start, you are more likely to continue.
- Try eliminating an item before you get a new one. After contemplating whether you can get that item, try eliminating something else that you are not using that much or at all. You may donate items you no longer use or resell them. You may want to keep a box on the side for things you no longer need, and once you have enough items, you can make one trip to the charity shop and donate.

After reading these tips, some readers would be able to begin planning. Others can require the help of a mentor, experienced organizer, or therapist to get started. If you need assistance, do not despair or give up. It took a lifetime to get to the state of disarray in which you have been living; it could take years to repair it. The important thing is to get started.

What Is ADHD

Are You Getting a Complete Picture of ADHD?

Overstimulation and under stimulation both affect executive functions, which means that overstimulation can lead to inattention and underemployment of brain resources. Under stimulation can also impact attention and work ethic if it doesn't lead to enough effort in response to the under-arousal, or relaxation response, associated with being bored.

Identifying ADHD is a process, and not everyone is helped by medication alone. In these cases, it's vital to have all of the tools you need to help your child succeed, which means knowing about his or her particular presentation and getting a complete assessment. The evaluation should include not only psychiatric interviews and questionnaires but also neuropsychological testing that can provide information about attention problems related to under- or overstimulation.

Understand Different Types of ADHD Presentations

ADHD must be diagnosed by a professional in order to receive appropriate treatment, but some practitioners are better at finding accurate diagnoses than others. Many of these professionals are referred to as "experts" rather than psychologists, but that doesn't mean they aren't trained in validating ADHD as a legitimate condition. There are several different types of ADHD presentations that can affect executive function and response to medication, and there's more to the condition than just hyperactivity and impulsivity.

ADHD with Over activity: Hyperactive-Impulsive Symptoms

Many people who have ADHD have hyperactive-impulsive symptoms that cause inattention as well. It's a common presentation that can cause considerable underachievement in school, and it often leads to social problems as well.

This means they're often less likely to get through college or complete work at a high level, and it can result in difficulty getting a job that is more than cleaning or serving customers.

Many people with these symptoms have an endless amount of energy but may lack the ability to focus on one thing for long enough to get anything done. A person with ADHD may be adept at cleaning a room, but if the task is boring or too taxing, he or she will get distracted and move onto something else.

Getting the right treatment can help with symptoms and help people with ADHD learn to differentiate tasks that require more concentration from those that don't. While medication can be effective for hyperactivity and impulsivity, talking therapies can help with inattention as well.

ADHD with Underemployment: Inattention

The symptoms of inattention can look a lot like the symptom of underachievement.

For example, a child may be able to answer questions in class and volunteer to answer them correctly, but she might not understand them or know how to apply the information that she's learning. She may be able to do her homework without any help and even get all of her assignments finished on time, but they might be incomplete or poorly done. This is often due to either a cognitive problem or an overreaction to stress—or both.

A child who has ADHD will need to have this addressed in order to succeed in school, though medication might be helpful with the underlying symptoms of impulsivity and hyperactivity.

ADHD with Disorganization: Proactive Symptoms, Inattention, and Underemployment

Proactive symptoms show up as problems with starting tasks or finishing them properly. You might notice that your child doesn't seem to know where things are in his or her room or wallet, or he or she might have trouble getting out the door on time. This can result in frustration and a sense of failure that spreads to other areas of life and can keep a person from succeeding socially as well as academically.

Being disorganized can also impact people's emotions. Organization can help people manage their time and plan for the day ahead. When someone feels that they're failing at this, it can cause them to feel a sense of helplessness that makes it difficult for them to deal with anything else in their lives. This leads to a cycle of failure and poor self-esteem, which makes it difficult for those with disorganization issues to find success in anything they do.

Many people who struggle with organization have trouble focusing on one thing for very long because there are always too many things to look at or worry about. It's important to keep your attention focused on one task and get that finished before moving onto something else.

If your child is struggling with these symptoms, it's important to talk to him or her about his or her thoughts and feelings. Asking questions like "What are you thinking about right now?" can help your child learn about his or her own thought process. This can help you help them break the cycle of failure, disorganization, and stress that is keeping them from succeeding in school or gaining a higher level of education than their current situation would seem to warrant.

Does ADHD Ever Go Away?

Ah, the joys of having ADHD. You know it's a laundry list of obstacles: social stigma, economic difficulty, inability to focus on anything for long periods of time... The list goes on and on. But you're not alone! In fact, about 10% of women in North America have this condition; there's no need to feel weird about it anymore.

And the good news is that yes, ADHD can go away. It's not a lifelong curse, and it's not a death sentence. The bad news? It can take time.

ADHD is a condition that affects many women, but it is not exclusive to women. Adults with ADHD have trouble with focus, organization, time management, and impulse control... And the disorder is marked by hyperactivity in childhood and a tendency toward inattention when they're older. Adults who have grown up with the effects of this disorder often struggle to deal with it; for some people, it's debilitating in relationships and career paths.

ADHD is not a death sentence, and it doesn't mean your child cannot be successful. Educate yourself about the disorder, and reach out to your local mental health organizations for more information. And don't forget to ask your doctor! The best way to understand a disorder like this is by getting the professional input that you need. ADHD can be managed with the correct treatment; when you seek help, you can eliminate the challenges that this condition brings about. It's worth it in the end — so take care of yourself today!

Is ADHD Inherited?

Much of ADHD, if not all of it, is inherited. A study done at Lafayette College in the United States found that in a sample of 700 adults with ADHD given a diagnosis by physicians, 95% had relatives with ADHD in their family history.

A study done at MIT came to the same conclusion about how much is inherited. The study found that "47 percent of women diagnosed with ADHD have an immediate family member also diagnosed.

A study done in Australia used both parents and women to measure ADHD in the family. The study concluded that 75% of the time, if both parents and women have ADHD, the child will have ADHD too.

The authors of this study said that "these findings indicate that a wide range of individually rare conditions can be quite common within families."

This means that many common problems can be shared by multiple members of a family. For example, there are many cases where one parent has depression or anxiety while another parent is having trouble keeping a job. The women in this family will have a much higher chance of having depression or anxiety and job problems.

A parent's emotional state can contribute to an ADHD child's emotional state. In the case of one study, high levels of cortisol, the stress hormone, were found in women with high levels of anxiety.

This might not be genetic but can be caused by a stressful environment where parents are arguing a lot or involved in other stressful events like a divorce. This can have negative effects on the child even if they don't share genes with their parents. The situation is stressful for the child and will cause them to have more cortisol than normal. Increased cortisol can cause ADHD like symptoms.

These include prenatal alcohol exposure, environmental toxicants such as lead, and maternal infections, nutrition and obesity before and during pregnancy. There are many other possible causes of ADHD that need to be taken into consideration if a child has ADHD. These include:

Studies have also shown that prenatal exposure to nicotine can increase the chances of a developing child becoming hyperactive and impulsive as well as affecting their ability to pay attention in school later in life.

One of the issues with ADHD is that there have been some cases where people have faked symptoms in order to get attention. One study found that 5% of the sample had malingered ADHD. This means that they lied about having ADHD in order to receive special treatment, which was seen as a positive result of their actions.

The only way to tell if someone has faked their ADHD diagnosis is a neuropsychological assessment by a highly trained professional. This is an expensive process and may not be worth it if the person isn't going to be seeking any professional help for his or her symptoms.

Many people are self-diagnosing, or "self-medicating", with ADHD and prescription medications. The use of these medications has become so common that they are being studied more often and it has even been reported in the scientific literature. In 2006 it was reported that over 50% of people who used psychostimulants for at least 6 months had received a diagnosis of ADHD by professionals. The reasons for the high rate of self-diagnosis are unknown.

As the use of ADHD medications increases, side effects such as weight loss and insomnia have become issues for many people who take them without understanding what they are putting into their bodies.

There is also a myth that ADHD is caused by poor nutrition. The evidence shows that this is not the case and it may have been started by unscrupulous doctors and commercial health providers who are trying to sell nutritional supplements as treatments for ADHD.

It is recommended that all caregivers give the same amount of attention to their women's needs. This includes spending time with the child, providing positive reinforcement and making sure that they have healthy nutrition and a safe play environment. These are all necessary for good development in women.

It is also important for adults with ADHD to combine treatment with positive parenting which can help manage their symptoms.

A 2008 study investigated parents' perception of parents' own functioning, as well as effects on their women's behaviors and performance in school when no diagnosis of ADHD is made or a diagnosis of ADHD is not made. The researchers used a measure called Parental Report of Disruptive Behavior (PRDB). The PRDB measures frequency of disruptive behavior reported by both mother and father. From this, the researchers calculated a total severity score. The higher the total severity score, the more severe the symptoms were in each parent.

Having ADHD may mean some difficulties for your child later on in life, but with assistance and patience it can be managed and even turned into an advantage some times. In the end, it doesn't matter if they have ADHD or not; it matters how they live their life and what they do with what they are given. The goal is for them to be happy and successful. You just want them to grow up feeling fulfilled no matter what path they take in life.

Having a child with ADHD can be a challenge, but it can also be very rewarding. Understanding the signs of ADHD will help you understand your child, which will in turn help you deal with her more effectively.

ADHD is not a wonderful disorder that should be "treated" like diabetes or high blood pressure or killed off like the common cold. It doesn't matter if she outgrows her ADHD -- if she doesn't live as well without it as she could have, it means something was wrong with how you raised her.

Some people think having ADHD is a badge of honor. Others struggle with a feeling of personal failure. Here are some facts about the disorder that will give you more useful information to make good parenting decisions in the future:

Limitations of ADHD Sufferers

ADHD is a mental disorder characterized by problems paying attention, excessive activity, and difficulty controlling behavior. While it primarily affects women and adolescent and about 4% of the population has ADHD, there are times that even adults can be afflicted with this disease. Unfortunately, many people don't know what to expect if they're diagnosed with ADHD. That's why we compiled this list of limitations for people who have been diagnosed with ADHD - as well as their loved ones - to better understand them.

It's difficult for an individual to complete tasks that require reading a long-form text such as books or novels due to their lack of attention span.

A person with ADHD tends to lose balance, which affects their ability to walk, run, and climb stairs.

A person with ADHD often loses things such as keys, wallets, credit cards or glasses.

That same individual can also misplace important documents such as bills or receipts. Addressed IEP Progress Reports (IDS) can be a good way to keep track of progress and help the teacher or parent know if goals are being met but they should not be your only way of keeping record of progress.

As adults, individuals with ADHD may be prone to alcohol and drug abuse because they are trying to self-medicate.

For this same reason, it is common for people with ADHD to have problems keeping friendships and intimate relationships.

Due to their lack of attention span, people with ADHD often suffer from short attention span. Reading or listening requires a lot of focus, so it's therefore not surprising if these individuals find it difficult to finish an entire article on the internet.

Since it's common for people with ADHD to get distracted, they may have a problem following instructions or timelines. It is important to be patient and understand that the individual is not intentionally trying to be difficult, but rather struggling to stay focused.

Individuals with ADHD are prone to mood swings, anxiety, and depression because they need consistency. If one topic is introduced and then something else starts instead, this can cause confusion in those with ADHD as they struggle to keep up.

Those who have symptoms of ADHD on the behavior side also frequently have symptoms of it on the emotional side such as feeling restless, moody or easily frustrated.

These individuals are often diagnosed with other disorders as well. Along with ADHD, it is not uncommon to be diagnosed with anxiety or depression, oppositional defiant disorder (ODD) or conduct disorder. It is a struggle for them to meet their potential if they live with so many limitations each day.

 The condition affects approximately 9-10% of school aged women, and even more adults who struggle to get through their daily routines due to a lack of concentration and focus.

It's no surprise why this is such a common condition; women today are busier and have so many distractions - from the TV to video games, to cell phones - that it is difficult for them to pay attention in class or focus at any task. For those with ADHD, they are often unaware of their condition. Adults can get diagnosed with ADHD when one of their women receives the diagnosis.

While this disease has many symptoms, there is no cure for it. The only thing that can be done to mitigate the disorder is to maintain a routine and set up reminders. This can include alarms on a cell phone, post-it notes and visual timetables. Another main point is to remember that you are not alone in this struggle.

Characteristics And Symptomatology

Women with ADHD will present with wide range of symptoms, including inattentiveness, distractibility, hyperactivity, and impulsiveness.

ADHD in women is different from ADHD in men; it can be subtler and masked. That's because there are fewer female role models for women who have attention disorders to look to for explanations or strategies to cope. Women are under more pressure than men — we're expected to "lead perfect lives" while simultaneously taking care of everyone else in our families. We often hold the responsibility as the primary caregiver as well as being a wife or mother.

Women with ADHD have unique issues from their male counterparts. Women may have greater difficulties with organization and multi-tasking. They tend to be more susceptible to feeling overwhelmed and out of control. Other characteristics that are likely to be present in women with ADHD include negative self-esteem, perfectionism, procrastination, mood swings, anxiety, and depression.

This may be because they do not seek treatment as often or because they are less likely to perceive themselves as having ADHD symptoms. Women with ADHD may feel confused and guilty as they watch their husbands, fathers or brothers having fun with their kids while they struggle to accomplish simple things like keeping the house clean, managing the children's schedules or meeting deadlines at work.

In order to overcome ADHD symptoms in women, it must first be recognized and diagnosed. Women need to remember that it is not uncommon for women to struggle with ADHD. Professional counselors are often trained in the symptoms of women's ADHD but sometimes have trouble diagnosing it due to lack of assistance from the patient. Because there are no outward signs of hyperactivity (running around) or impulsiveness (quick temper) in women, there is difficulty identifying symptoms and making a diagnosis. Because women tend to be more in tune with their children, husbands or families than they are with themselves, they may be unaware of the disruptive behavior that is affecting their lives. A family member or loved one may have noticed first how a woman's behavior was causing difficulty for the family, but she may have overlooked these warning signs.

Upon diagnosis, Women can take many routes of treatment for ADHD. The most common routes involve medication and counseling. Depending on a patient's preference and which symptoms she is trying to combat, she can choose to take stimulants (Adderall), or non-stimulants (Strattera). Most women will take a combination of the two.

Women with ADHD tend to have less success with behavioral therapy than men. This is because it is harder for women than men to verbalize their feelings and talk about themselves in a group setting. Women are generally more comfortable alone; they often find being in a group stressful and conflict-laden, and they are less able to voice their own opinions due to social pressures. The nurturing instincts of women make them excellent counselors, but these same instincts make them poor candidates for counseling or therapy. In order to overcome this hurdle, counselors should be trained specifically in women's issues regarding ADHD. It is equally important for women with ADHD to be aware of their feelings and be able to put them into words.

Aside from counseling, women should also be encouraged to create a network of friends who understand and support them. Because women's issues with ADHD may not be apparent in everyday conversation, it is often easier for the patient and her friends to discuss ADHD anonymously through email or chat rooms. Support groups can also be beneficial for women with ADHD. They allow the patient to share thoughts and ideas with others who have the same issues as well as provide a social outlet among other women who understand how they feel.

Women can learn ways to cope by talking with others about their options. They can learn ways to help themselves avoid or overcome the symptoms they are having, as well as being able to identify the symptoms that others have that may be of an ADHD nature. A positive attitude is key to overcoming and coping with ADHD for women.

It's estimated that about 5% of women have ADHD. Many people, including women themselves, don't know they have it because it is a disorder that often goes undiagnosed. Symptoms can include trouble concentrating and staying on task, impulsive behavior, interrupting others while they speak and an inability to follow directions. When picking up small pieces of clothing from the floor or putting around the house putting items away might seem like work in comparison with a task at work that may be more stimulating but provides less satisfaction.

Women can start showing symptoms as early as childhood and sometimes the problem doesn't come to light until they are adults. Symptoms of inattentive ADHD in women might include difficulties staying organized, keeping track of time, following a schedule. They may have trouble concentrating on a specific topic in conversation or reading interesting books or engaging friends in conversations that require more than just a few words. Women with ADHD also can have problems with organization, procrastination and time management. They may have trouble meeting deadlines or remembering to do things, such as paying bills or returning calls. Trouble sticking to a daily routine is another common problem. Having not completed a project or task by the deadline they are often late in submitting work for school or at the office.

Women who suffer from ADHD sometimes also struggle with depression, eating disorders, anxiety and substance abuse problems. Because women are often socialized to be caregivers, they may be too easily distracted by family matters when trying to complete tasks at work that need their full attention (e.g., answering calls from home, talking with coworkers about personal issues).

Symptoms of ADHD

If you are struggling with any of the following symptoms, it is likely that you have ADHD.

- Strong sense of self-identity
- Fidgeting behavior or impulsivity, especially in the classroom or workplace
- Easily bored and seeking activities that stimulate interest
- Difficulty remaining attentive (can't seem to pay attention for more than two consecutive minutes)
- Impulsiveness (e.g. blurting out answers in school, interrupting a conversation, or blurting out ideas at the dinner table)
- Trouble waiting their turn
- Often talk too much
- Difficulties with paying attention and following through with instructions and directions
- Difficulty starting tasks, making decisions, or finishing tasks
- Engaging in multiple conversations at once (e.g. text messaging while listening to a speaker).
- Having a short attention span and flitting from one subject to another, one activity to another.
- Blurting out comments or answers in class, rushing through homework assignments, not completing projects or chores.
- Lack of organization (e.g. making careless mistakes while preparing for assignments, leaving things undone at home or work, or forgetting to bring something with them when they leave their room)
- Difficulty keeping a schedule and following through on tasks (e.g. skipping breakfast, missing appointments)
- Repeating routines until they are perfect (e.g., playing catch-up after being behind on homework; getting dressed and ready for school several times each day; needing to do homework over and over until it is complete)
- Having difficulty organizing their thoughts and direction (e.g. not knowing what to say in a conversation, not being able to recall information they learned in the past, and difficulty making decisions)

- Having a difficult time shifting from one activity to another (e.g. From homework you go straight to dinner and then jump right into sports practice)
- Having trouble relaxing (e.g. working out or doing homework until the wee morning hours)
- Frequently losing their way or forgetting daily routines (e.g., forgetting to stop at the grocery store on the way home from work or school; requiring reminders to take out the trash)
- Getting so deeply involved with an activity that it can interfere with their health, appetite, sleep, or regular daily activities (e.g. working out, reading, playing video/computer games, or watching TV)
- Being embarrassed or reluctant to sit still when required by a classroom teacher
- Having trouble keeping their balance while sitting or standing (e.g. they are often bumping into things or running into people)
- Getting more restless and unable to concentrate when they are required to stay still for a period of time (e.g. during a movie)
- Acting without thinking (e.g., buying something without considering the consequences; starting conversations without thinking about what they might say; approaching dangerous situations without considering the consequence; jumping from one activity to another and never finishing anything).
- Speaking before thinking (e.g., sharing too much information; blurting out something negative about someone or a group of people)
- Lacking empathy for others
- Frequently being ridiculed, teased, or bullied by peers
- Having difficulty describing or putting words to their feelings, often mistaking their feelings for someone else's
- Acting before they think (e.g., rushing into dangerous situations without considering the consequences).

Causes Of ADHD

ADHD is a developmental disorder that makes it hard for people to pay attention and control their behavior. The causes of ADHD are still not well understood, but research has shown that the following factors increase the likelihood of developing this disorder: family history, genetics, brain abnormalities, prenatal exposure to alcohol or tobacco, and environmental toxins.

There are different types of attention deficits such as short-term memory (which means forgetting what happened a few minutes ago), sustained attention (tending to lose focus after some time), difficulty with organization and planning (making lists or alphabetizing papers), ability to shift between tasks or activities (poor multi-tasking skills) and an inability to ignore distractions.

Children with ADHD may be overactive, talk excessively, act recklessly or impulsively (without thinking about consequences), and have difficulty remaining seated when required.

Attention deficit hyperactivity disorder co-occurs with other mental health disorders such as anxiety disorders (including social phobia), oppositional defiant disorder, conduct disorder or substance use and dependence. Children with ADHD are at risk for injuries and accidents, which often leads to involvement in the legal system.

Genetics

ADHD is a highly inheritable disorder. If one of your parents has ADHD, it is likely that you will develop the disorder too. That is because the condition tends to run in families. Researchers believe there is a dominant gene (apart from one copy) that transmits this illness to offspring. They are also uncovering some of the precise genetic differences related to ADHD. Still, environmental factors seem to play a significant role in the onset of the disorder.

Brain Abnormalities

Abnormalities in brain structures are linked to an increased risk of developing attention deficit hyperactivity disorder (ADHD) in children. Researchers have found several areas of the brain different in people with ADHD as compared to those without the condition. These areas include the anterior cingulate cortex, which is involved in regulation or inhibition of behaviors; the caudate nucleus, which is related to executive functioning and impulse control; and the cerebellum, which is involved in motor control including eye movements. The increased activity occurring in these regions may explain why it's hard for someone with ADHD to pay attention or remain focused on one thing.

Prenatal Exposure to Alcohol and/or Tobacco

Children whose mothers drank alcohol during pregnancy are at greater risk of developing ADHD than children whose mothers did not.

Tobacco use also appears to increase the risk of ADHD among children. The higher the level of smoking in a mother, the greater the chance her child will develop this disorder. It is not known whether this is caused by chemicals in tobacco smoke or by other unhealthy choices that parents who smoke also make, such as drinking more alcohol or eating poorly.

Environmental Toxins

Certain chemicals that are found in the environment may have a role in the development of ADHD. For example, researchers have shown that lead blocks a chemical in the brain called dopamine, which is linked to attention and behavior. Some studies suggest a link between prenatal exposure to polychlorinated biphenyls (PCBs), which are industrial chemicals, and increased risk for ADHD although it is very difficult to determine whether PCBs cause this health problem.

As scientists learn more about how ADHD affects children, they will gain new insights into accurate diagnosis and effective ways to treat it.

Difference Between ADD and ADHD

ADHD is the attention deficit hyperactivity disorder, which is an impairment of the brain. It means that a person cannot focus on one task for more than a few minutes at a time. The ADHD brain has difficulty filtering out distractions and so it can be very difficult to work on school or job tasks without becoming bored or restless.

ADD stands for Attention Deficit Disorder and refers to what used to be called "minimal brain dysfunction" in children and adults before ADHD was identified as their specific condition. ADD also makes it hard for people to focus on tasks, but they can stay focused for hours at a time if they are doing something that interests them. The ADD brain may have some lower level of functioning, such as a poor memory or a delay in learning, but the individual usually has the mental capacity to function at an average level.

The key is that people with ADD are not lazy or irresponsible; they simply have a hard time controlling their behavior and emotions when things are out of control. If adults with ADD are doing the same things they always do, it's not a disorder; it's daydreaming or procrastination. Being impulsive can be an asset for many careers, but people with this condition need to learn to manage their impulses before they hurt themselves badly or others.

In situations where the person with ADD is feeling good about themselves, they will perform at a high level and are generally able to control their impulses. It is when they are feeling bad that they become impulsive and lose touch with reality. They may suffer from depression, which can make it hard to do well in school or at a job. The job of the neuropsychologist is to help people like this through therapy, management of medication, as well as corrective psychological exercises. The trick is linking the specific difficulty to its cause so that therapy can target that specific area of weakness.

A neuropsychologist who has specialized training in treating people with brain impairment knows how to repair the identified deficits and get them back on track again. Some of the exercises used are memory games to improve the quality of a person's thinking, especially in dealing with details and numbers. After doing this for several sessions, they may find it easier to stay focused on one task. If there is a problem in paying attention while reading or studying, they can learn to break the reading material into smaller pieces that are more easily absorbed.

Since people with ADD often have problems with time management, their therapist will teach them how to plan and manage their activities over the course of the day. They may also need help taking notes at meetings or lectures and keeping track of assignments while staying organized at home. Finally, they need some strategies to help them deal with the insomnia and anxiety that go hand-in-hand with this condition. When they can stay focused and complete their work, they will discover that it is not an impairment.

In all likelihood, ADD was not diagnosed when you were a child. It is a new concept and may have been thought of as daydreaming or laziness in your younger years. In fact, researchers found that 30% of adults with ADHD suffered from other disorders as children including depression, learning disabilities or anxiety. Children are often misdiagnosed as having behavioral problems when what's really going on is an impairment in their ability to focus and concentrate long enough to complete a task. They may also have learning disabilities and other problems in school or other settings.

These conditions are treated with a holistic approach that combines medication, therapy, education and rehabilitation to integrate you into your work or school environment. Other approaches such as cognitive behavior therapy (CBT) can be used to treat the anxiety and depression associated with this disorder. CBT teaches people how to deal with their emotions by recognizing them and changing how they think about the situations that are causing them stress.

The key is for you to understand yourself better so that you can control your impulses and feel more comfortable in social environments, at work or at home. Some people with ADHD are also gifted and creative, so you may be surprised by their achievements when they have the skills to bring out their abilities. Previous generations of people who experienced a similar type of brain impairment were labeled as having minimal brain damage or feeblemindedness. The neuropsychologist is here to help you rise above the negative connotations of those outdated labels.

Seeking help from a neuropsychologist means that you are taking control of your life instead of living with an impairment that may be preventing you from reaching your potential as a human being, spouse or parent. A joint counseling effort will identify the important role that ADD plays in your life and help you build a better future fitted to your strengths and limitations. Neuropsychological testing is the best way to isolate the specific problem areas that need to be treated and help you build your life and business on a stronger foundation.

The Three Variations Of ADHD

One of the most common disorders that we see in children is Attention Deficit Hyperactivity Disorder (ADHD). This disorder has three variations and each has a different set of symptoms. The three types are attention deficit disorder without hyperactivity, attention deficit disorder with hyperactivity, and ADHD combined type.

It might be hard to believe, but there are three different types of ADHD. The first type is Predominantly Inattentive, the second type is Predominantly Hyperactive/Impulsive and the third type is a combination of both with an uneven effect on inattention and impulsivity.

Since each person has a unique symptom profile, it's difficult to know which type you have without doing a clinical assessment. Luckily for the rest of us though (or maybe not so luckily), it's not uncommon for someone to exhibit symptoms from multiple types over their lifetime.

The two hyperactive-impulsive types are easier to recognize because they generally present one way throughout childhood and into adulthood: the person is either hyperactive, or impulsive. Meanwhile, the inattentive type is much subtler and difficult to recognize. They don't have the outward characteristics of ADHD that people generally associate with hyperactivity, but rather are disorganized and distant from other people.

There's also the combination type, where someone has a combination of symptoms from both categories. Because of this, it's harder to tell which type they are.

There are also some other distinguishing characteristics that researchers have found can help show up in blood tests, but if you don't have them or they don't apply to you, there's not much point in worrying about them. They include:

Difficulty maintaining attention (impulsivity) problems regulating emotions (inattention)

Difficulty with organization and planning (hyperactivity) a pattern of careless mistakes (both in attention and impulsivity)

The three types are based on the way people respond to stimulant medications. So far, many people who end up being diagnosed with ADHD are diagnosed due to their negative behavior. But when people who had been diagnosed with ADHD but weren't taking medication were asked to take stimulant medication and were told it would also help with their mood, they responded much more positively than they had without the knowledge that their mood would improve.

This is most likely because of the symptoms that allow someone to know whether or not they have ADHD in the first place. For example, ADHD doesn't generally present with a person's left eye twitching or their hands shaking. People who have ADHD often get much better grades than people without it, although having ADHD can interfere with the kind of work they do in school. Their personal relationships are often very difficult as well.

ADHD is diagnosed when a child or adult has at least 5 of 11 symptoms from the DSM-IV criteria and shows significant impairment in two or more settings (including school, home and work environment). The 11 symptoms are:

In Predominantly Inattentive Type:

- Often fails to give close attention to details or makes careless mistakes in schoolwork, work, etc.

- Often has difficulty sustaining attention in tasks or play activities.
- Often does not seem to listen when spoken to directly.
- Often has difficulty organizing tasks and activities.
- Often loses things necessary for tasks and activities (e.g., toys, school assignments, pencils, books, or tools).
- Is often easily distracted by extraneous stimuli.
- Is often forgetful in daily activities.
- Often avoids, dislikes, or is reluctant to engage in tasks that require sustained mental effort (such as schoolwork or homework).
- In Predominantly Hyperactive/Impulsive Type:
- Often has difficulty playing quietly.
- Often interrupts or intrudes on others (e.g., butts into conversations or games).
- Often "multitasks" or engages in several conversations or activities at once.
- Often has trouble waiting his/her turn.
- Often shifts from one activity to another without finishing what was started.
- Often does not follow through on instructions.
- Is often "on the go" and act without thinking, such as being able to multi-task, stay on task, or start something and then not finish it (but may be able to restart after a delay).
- In Combination Type:
- Often fidgets with hands or feet or squirms in seat.
- Often has difficulty playing quietly.
- Often interrupts or intrudes on others (e.g., butts into conversations or games).
- Often "multitasks" or engages in several conversations or activities at once.
- Often has trouble waiting his/her turn.
- Often shifts from one activity to another without finishing what was started.

Relational Problems and Comorbidity

One of the most common misconceptions about women with ADHD is that they are unable to maintain relationships. In fact, adults with ADHD often make great partners because they are compassionate and care deeply about their relationships.

GETTING ALONG WITH PEOPLE is something that many individuals with ADHD do quite well. The energy, spontaneity, empathy, humor, and creativity that are common to many people with ADHD create a certain level of charm that comes across in a positive way to other people. Many adults with ADHD are attracted to each other on the basis of these positive personal qualities.

The personal qualities that make a person with ADHD a fun date can also make her or him a very loving spouse, partner, or parent. As is often the case, in a marriage or other long-term relationship some less positive aspects of ADHD biology can and do cause difficulties and challenges at times. These are not typically insurmountable challenges, but they may need some work. Just like any other relationships.

Let's be very clear about one thing: it is always the responsibility of the person with ADHD to be responsible for their own behavior and to do what they need to do. Responsible people do not make excuses, and ADHD should never be used as an excuse for not fulfilling one's responsibilities. Just like everyone else.

Common Issues in Personal Relationships

Difficulty Listening and Paying Attention

An individual with a high level of distractibility is more likely to "zone out" during a conversation. This is pure biology, not volitional behavior. Problems arise if the other partner interprets the behavior as a sign of indifference or disrespect. Hey, I'm talking to you – don't you care about what I have to say?

The fact of the matter is that the person does care, but there will be times when his or her mind will wander. When that happens simply point it out, and she or he will "snap out of it" and be attentive again.

Understanding the biology of distractibility helps in not taking the behavior personally and feeling slighted or rejected.

Another communication issue that can cause bad feelings and friction is when the person frequently interrupts in conversation. This leads to "talking over" the other person.

This impulsive behavior is sometimes caused by the ADHD partner getting excited about an idea or thought they want to express – and boom, can't wait, and out it comes! At times the ADHD partner may be worried that they will forget what they want to say – and bam, they just go ahead and say it.

If these behaviors get irritating over time, as can happen with any couple and irritating behavior, they should be treated as communication issues and addressed accordingly. As always, the partner with ADHD should be responsible and considerate and make efforts to be attentive and to tone down the impulsivity

Trouble Completing Tasks

Not following through and doing what one is expected to do always create feelings of frustration. Sometimes it leads to resentment and anger. Knowing that a person keeps their promises is one of the foundations of trust.

In every relationship each person is responsible for following through and doing her or his share of the work. This may be as simple as taking out the garbage on a regular basis, or as complicated as planning next year's vacation trip to Europe. Do what you agree to do.

Problems arise when one person is not consistent in doing their share. A common pattern is that the other partner becomes the one who has to remind often, then eventually nag, then perhaps occasionally threaten. In a very toxic dynamic the partners take on a parent-child role.

Forgetfulness

Everyone forgets. People with ADHD tend to be more forgetful than most people. This is also pure biology; however, that does not make it any less frustrating when it keeps happening excessively. Two things can help, one to a small degree and one to a very large degree.

What can help to a small degree is for the non-ADHD partner to be careful not to interpret forgetfulness on the part of the person with ADHD as a lack of caring or lack of commitment to the relationship. Forgetfulness is biology, and it is not related to intelligence or caring.

What can help to a very large degree (and really is the only solution to this problem) is for the partner with ADHD to work diligently on designing and then using a system of organization and reminders, do that, and important things are not forgotten or neglected. It is the only responsible way to manage forgetfulness.

Emotional Overreaction

The level of emotionality for many people with ADHD is simply higher than for people in the general population. That can be a double-edged sword. On the positive side it can make people more caring, more loving, more passionate about things that interest them, and more committed to things they believe in.

On the negative side, it can make some people more likely to overreact emotionally. That might mean that people get upset too easily, are irritated or bothered by minor things, or lose their temper too quickly. Some people have a greater sensitivity to criticism, disapproval, or rejection. Very emotional people react very emotionally.

One solution to emotional over-reactivity is to de-fuse when possible, and also to refuse to escalate. This might mean acknowledging the upset feelings but then, if the anger persists, distancing from it. Ask that you take some time to cool down and then discuss the matter. One positive thing about ADHD emotionality is that while people are likely to get upset quickly, they are also likely to get over it quickly.

Not Staying in Touch with Old Friends (And New)

 "Out of sight, out of mind" is a problem that applies to friends as well as objects and tasks. Many people with ADHD get so caught up in the present they don't think about taking the time to call or write old friends, plan a get together, and send a birthday card, and so on. Making friends? Easy, maintaining friendships? More difficult

Common Issues in Professional Relationships

Procrastination

Procrastination is always perceived by supervisors and co-workers as irresponsible, unmotivated, and simply "lazy." It has no redeeming positive qualities. It hurts productivity for the individual, and for the team the person is working on. If excessive, it gets people fired.

Difficulties with Planning and Organization

A disorganized workplace is not only bad for efficiency and productivity but is viewed by many as an indication of a sloppy and uncaring attitude. Inconsistent and disorganized effort, jumping around from one thing to another, shows lack of planning and discipline and is always viewed as unprofessional.

Lack of Punctuality

Late for meetings, late in completing tasks. Late for lunch, I'm late, I'm late, and I'm late

Tardiness always comes across in a negative way. Yes, even if people joke about it. It often inconveniences other people, and always looks irresponsible. If lack of punctuality is a chronic problem, it may be time to do more work on time management skills.

Being Intrusive or Disruptive

Most people with ADHD do not tolerate boredom well. As children they might become the "class clown," or disrupt the class by excessive talking to other people around them. As adults, sometimes these social and disruptive behaviors pop up in a work setting. It is imperative to be attentive to social cues that indicate the person in question does not welcome the attention at that point in time.

We often describe the behavior of ADHD as impulsive, disorganized, violent, overly reactive, intense, emotional, or destructive. In their social world, their social experiences with others — parents, relatives, teachers, peers, co-workers, spouses/partners — are always fraught with confusion and miscommunication. Those with ADHD have a diminished capacity to self-regulate their behavior and responses towards others. That can lead to overly strained and fragile relationships [67]

Social Skills in Adults with ADHD

People with ADHD also encounter social challenges as a consequence of their inattention, impulsiveness, and hyperactivity, social rejection, and interpersonal relationship issues. Such interpersonal, adverse effects cause both mental distress and suffering. These also tend to exist with co-morbid mood disorders and anxiety disorders. Since there is very little research on social skills in adults with ADHD, the suggestions given in this book are focused primarily on sound clinical practices and upward extrapolations from research on social skills and ADHD for children.

The Overall Effect of ADHD on Social Interactions

The reasons why people with ADHD frequently struggle in social settings are not difficult to grasp. Some of the most critical aspects of a child's development are to connect with peers and significant adults actively, but 50 to 60 percent of children with ADHD have trouble with peer relationships. More than 25 percent of Americans experience persistent isolation. [68] One can only guess that adults with ADHD are much higher in number.

Over time, these derogatory labels lead to a person with ADHD being socially rejected. Social rejection creates emotional distress in the lives of many of the children and adults who have ADHD and, in their life, may trigger confusion and lower self-esteem. Your improper social conduct may annoy your partner or spouse in relationships and marriages, which may ultimately "burn out" and give up on the relationship or marriage. Educating yourself, your significant others, and your peers about ADHD and the ways it affects social skills and behavioral habits will help reduce much of the tension and blame. With a proper diagnosis, care, and education, you may learn to communicate with others in a way that improves your social life successfully.

ADHD and Social Skills Development

You typically learn social skills incidentally: watching others, observing others' behaviors, performing, and getting input. Some people begin this process early in their infancy. Social skills are learned and developed while "playing grown-up" and other events of childhood. Children with ADHD often overlook many of these nuanced behaviors. They may pick up bits and pieces of what's right, but they lack a general understanding of social standards. Sadly, they still know that "something" is lacking as adults but are never quite sure what this "something" maybe. We can define social acceptance as a continuum of ups and downs. We reward individuals with appropriate social skills with greater recognition from those they communicate with and are motivated to acquire even better social skills. The spiral also goes down for someone with ADHD. Their lack of social skills leads to friend's rejection, which then restricts social skills learning opportunities, leading to further rejection, and so on. Social punishment involves rejection, avoidance, and other, less overt ways of expressing disapproval to one another.

It's important to remember that you may not be made aware of your mistakes. Society considers it socially unacceptable to point out a social competence mistake. Consequently, you may be left alone, trying to develop your social skills without knowing precisely what areas need to be changed.

- Tension and dispute are common in marriages and partnerships that involve a person with ADHD. Individuals with ADHD are frequently forgetful, disorganized, distracted, reckless, and interact poorly and overreact emotionally due to the deficiencies in executive performance, inhibitory control, and attention mechanisms associated with ADHD. And if the ADHD is undiagnosed, there is no context in which either partner can recognize these traits, and these behaviors can elicit adverse responses and blameful attributions from the partner without ADHD. [73]

The ADHD-free spouse can perceive poor communication, emotional outbursts, and failure to fulfill commitments as proof that the ADHD spouse does not care about or support the person without ADHD. All derive negative conclusions about each other's intentions and actions, which intensify constant tension, poor behavioral habits, and inadequate dispute resolution strategies, ultimately endangering the relationship. The inefficient executive brain functions of the person with ADHD are further exacerbated by the added obligations of home and children. [74]

- Doesn't recall being told things
- Says things without thought
- 'Zones out' in discussions
- Has difficulty coping with frustration
- Has difficulty getting started on a task

- Underestimates the time required to complete a task
- Leaves a mess
- Doesn't complete household tasks.

Resolution and the healing start with the consciousness of the pair to distinguish the individual from the condition. You may need to get a mental health professional assessment and/or treatment. Couples / marital counseling can also be effective.

Though women are generally better at "multi-tasking" than men, many neuroscientists say that this trait is hardwired in the female brain. The neurotransmitters that drive women to juggle many tasks also make it difficult for them to focus on a single activity or conversation for long periods of time.

Attention deficit disorder (ADD) and attention deficit hyperactivity disorder (ADHD) are believed to affect 30 million Americans, including 10% of all schoolchildren. Women—who generally score higher than men on tests measuring inattention and impulsivity—suffer more frequently from these conditions than male counterparts. ADD is considered one of the most common neurological disorders among children, with boys and girls affected equally. But by adulthood, the numbers are reversed; women are much more likely to show impaired executive functioning than men.

Studies among adults suggest that inattention isn't always an obstacle to success and happiness. In fact, some researchers argue that people with ADHD tend to have more friends and better social skills than those who don't have the disorder. Studies have also found a positive relationship between ADHD symptoms—such as distractibility and forgetfulness—and creativity in both men and women. In addition, people with ADHD may be more imaginative or open-minded when it comes to solving problems or seeing new possibilities for a situation.

Many adults with ADHD have had lifelong relationships and stable employment, but these are typically unfulfilling because of difficulty maintaining focus in a long-term relationship. For instance, people with ADHD may be attracted to other people who are impulsive and crave high risk, even though the thrill of new experiences lasts only a few hours or days.

"Managing the "big picture", the whole relationship, is very difficult for those with ADHD," writes Christine A. Dolman in "ADHD: Truth Behind the Myth".

Children with ADHD may also have difficulty resolving problems peacefully. For most people, verbalizing a problem is a step in finding a solution. But for children with ADHD, the act of naming the problem or its cause can make it more difficult to find a solution. These children are often overly emotional and aggressive when they're upset; as they get older, they may take out their frustrations on peers and family members in unhealthy ways.

Relationships are generally made up of give and take. People with ADHD tend to focus on their own needs rather than consider how their actions will affect others, which can make it difficult to maintain good relationships over time. As they get older, children with ADHD may lose friends because of their inappropriate behaviors, and spouses may leave because of the erratic parenting.

Some researchers believe that adolescents with ADHD are more likely to be dismissed by teachers and classmates and to avoid participation in extracurricular activities since these are not skill based. Teens with ADHD maintain relationships in isolation rather than face-to-face interactions with other people.

According to one survey, there's a reason why adults with ADHD may have more difficulty than others in keeping friends and relationships. Adults with ADHD tend to have many of the same limitations as children, including problems working independently; disorganization; forgetting details about a conversation or agreement; failing to finish tasks; and the inability to keep promises.

Many adults try to hide their symptoms from their partner until they become extreme. They're afraid that if they admit having these symptoms, they'll be judged as "lazy." But the truth is that people with ADHD want relationships and are often willing to do whatever it takes—sometimes with professional help—to achieve them.

"I find that the majority of people I work with have a fairly high functioning ability to sit down and talk with me, and to understand what we're doing," says Ken Blum, PhD, author of "Oppositional Defiant Disorder: A Guide for Adults". "One thing we have trouble with is conveying in words how difficult it is for us to do this."

Perhaps the most important element in sustaining a relationship is communication. There's no way around it—even people who don't suffer from ADHD need to learn how to communicate effectively.

Communication Tips for People with ADHD

1. Work on being a good listener.
2. Tell your partner what you're feeling without attacking him or her. "I feel unimportant when you leave the house without telling me where you're going," is much more effective than, "You never tell me what's going on!"
3. Use "I" messages (i.e., I feel..., I need..., etc.). This distancing helps avoid defensiveness and promotes a more open dialogue between both partners.
4. Use "I" messages when you're asking for changes in your partner, too. Saying, "I feel more comfortable if you would ask before you go out with the guys," can be helpful.
5. Use active listening techniques such as reflecting and summarizing what your partner says or repeating back what your partner has said in a different way to make sure that the message was understood correctly.
6. Be an active listener (not just a passive one) when your partner talks about ADHD symptoms or his or her concerns. Don't offer advice unless it's asked for; simply listen and validate (don't judge).
7. If you don't understand what your partner is saying, ask him or her to explain more clearly.
8. Be aware of how you react to your partner's behavior and try to practice patience and understanding.
9. Don't confuse assertiveness with aggression. It's okay for you to let others know when you're unhappy about

something, but it's not okay for you to be verbally abusive or critical of others' thoughts and feelings.

10. Use "I" statements when asking for a change in your partner (i.e., "I need more attention."). This will help avoid blaming the other person while still expressing how his or her actions affect you.

11. Know when it's appropriate to discuss ADHD, and to whom. You probably don't want to talk about your partner's symptoms or medication use with every person you meet.

12. Understand that the issues that cause conflict in your relationship are not related to ADHD alone; they're also a result of the way in which both partners are communicating. Working on improving your communication skills is just as important as using medications and learning coping strategies for ADHD symptoms and behaviors.

Anxiety and ADHD

It's estimated that up to 40% of women in the United States suffer from ADHD and anxiety. Women with ADHD often struggle in school, have trouble with work and relationships, experience difficulties with socializing, and find themselves constantly distracted by their thoughts. Women also struggle with anxiety due to social media use or family dynamics.

This will explore how women coping with those conditions can make changes to their lives for the better while navigating through life's challenges.

Anxiety is the most common mental health issue in the United States. It's estimated that 40 million people, just over 18% of the population, deal with anxiety. Anxiety is a wide category that covers a range of issues from everyday stress and worry to severe phobias and obsessive-compulsive disorder (OCD). Common symptoms of anxiety include muscle tension, racing thoughts, racing heartbeat, difficulty concentrating, and restlessness.

Anxiety can be brought on by innate factors like genetic predisposition or trauma or acquired through life experiences like bereavement or social isolation. Like ADHD women with anxiety often have trouble functioning at school or work and struggle in relationships due to their inability to concentrate on tasks or keep still.

Anxiety is often treated with medication. Selective serotonin reuptake inhibitors (SSRIs) like bupropion, duloxetine, citalopram and sertraline are examples of the most commonly prescribed anti-anxiety medications.

Food allergies are also a source of anxiety for many people. Food sensitivities and intolerances can bring on the same symptoms that people with anxiety suffer from without the need for medication or therapy. Nutrient deficiencies can lead to reduced serotonin levels and research has shown that supplementing with amino acid L-Tryptophan can reduce anxiety symptoms in some patients.

ADHD is the most common mental disorder in children and adults and affects over 13 million people just in the United States. ADHD is hereditary; it is thought that genetics play a large role in about 75% of cases. However, low levels of dopamine do not properly explain all cases. About 75% of ADHD patients are male with 5% being diagnosed before adulthood and 20% being diagnosed after school age.

There are many women with Attention Deficit Hyperactivity Disorder and Anxiety who struggle to find ways to live full and happy lives. With the right guidance, they can find a way through their challenges. Adapt these tips into your daily life in order to take back control of your life and live a fuller, happier day-to-day life.

Women with ADHD and Anxiety often feel like they can't do enough for themselves. This boredom leads to depression and anxiety. There are many ways to help this. Start by setting small goals. Let's say you're bored with the way your room is set up. Start by making your bed, then putting away clothes, or whatever you feel the need for. Set a timer when you start and do not move on to something else until that time has passed. Then reward yourself with ten minutes of free time, an episode of to, etc.

The more you force yourself to stick with one task at a time; the easier it becomes over time. If you are a closet loser and don't like confrontation or the way you look, dress yourself up. Do not focus on perfection but rather show yourself that you are a successful woman with ADHD and Anxiety. A nice pair of earrings can make the difference between having one bad day and being in a rut.

Many women with ADHD know that working out can be difficult for them. Often times it is not possible for them to go to the gym or do yoga on their own schedule and sometimes it's just too hard to fit it in with work and school. This can be very frustrating for them. Working out with a partner, an exercise buddy, or just doing it on your own is a great way to beat this frustration.

Many women with ADHD and Anxiety are not capable of planning their day, but they know what they need for the most part. Plan small goals in order to get yourself through the day or week. Don't forget to reward yourself periodically and then keep doing it until you reach your new goal!

Many people have discussed how stresses pile on one another. This can lead to serious anxiety issues in women with ADHD and Anxiety. Have designated times during the week when you can do absolutely nothing.

Women with ADHD and Anxiety are often very good at multi-tasking. They can often handle multiple things at once; but this also leads them to be scattered and a little all over the place. This can lead to lack of focus, poor performance at school or work, and just overall chaos in your life. If you want to live a simpler life, then start by regulating your schedule during the week.

This will help you stay focused on one task at a time instead of having everything coming at once. You will also be able to find more time for yourself in other areas of your life. This can lead to less anxiety, less stress, and just overall happiness in you. If you have a partner or family, set aside a day when they don't have to be around. Make another day the "family" day or "partner" day.

Many people with ADHD do not get enough sleep on a regular basis and this can cause more anxiety and depression than normal. Be sure to make your bedtime routines just that; routines. Keep the same time everyday so that your body clock will be able to fall asleep when it's supposed to without any problems.

This also allows you time to wind down before bed. Make sure all electronics, including your phone, are out of the bedroom. This will help lessen the amount of anxiety you get in a night. During this time, make sure you run any errands that might be needed or complete any tasks for the next day before you go to bed. This will allow you to wake up refreshed and relaxed instead of rushed and stressed.

Depression and ADHD

Women with ADHD and depression face a unique set of challenges—and often cope with them in entirely new ways.

A lot of the time, it's hard to tell if these two conditions are at work independently or together. We talked to three women who have ADHD and depression. all diagnosed late in life, for their perspectives on how these disorders manifest themselves differently in female-identifying individuals.

Women with ADHD are six times more likely to have depression. Women with ADHD experience greater impairment in many areas of their lives, report negative self-esteem, and are more often diagnosed as having other types of mental illness than men.

The information provided might be helpful for people looking for a reason why their partner shows signs of depression and/or hyperactivity.

It can also help individuals who have been diagnosed with either condition, or both, and want to understand the other in order to have a more accurate understanding of themselves and those around them.

It can offer support for friends and family members as well as sufferers themselves.

Research has shown that women with ADHD are more likely to have been depressed than those without ADHD. Women with ADHD are also more likely to have anxiety, eating disorders, substance abuse and personality disorders. These women often experience relationship problems, as well as difficulties in holding a job and financial difficulties. When accounting for co-existing depression, however, the negative impact of this group on employment was not found to be any different from those without ADHD.

While men with ADHD were more likely to be diagnosed with conduct disorder (CD), antisocial personality disorder (ASPD), violent tendencies and alcoholism than women, those who had been diagnosed with CD as children are three times more likely to commit crimes than men without this diagnosis.

When a study was done comparing treatment for ADHD in men and women, the women were less likely to respond to therapy.

Women with ADHD score higher on scales of depression than do men with the disorder. Women are more than twice as likely to be depressed compared to men with ADHD. Women also have greater rates of eating disorders and anxiety disorders than those without ADHD. In addition, they experience more marital conflict and hostility than do men with and without ADHD.

In a study of ADHD in adults, the frequency of alcohol problems was higher among those with ADHD, specifically for women. Approximately one in four women with ADHD have a drinking problem compared to only one in ten men with the disorder.

Elevated rates of suicidal behavior in children have been reported for boys and girls who meet criteria for hyperactive-impulsive and combined subtypes of ADHD; however, no such pattern is seen in adolescents and adults. One study report that adults with ADHD are more likely to commit suicide than adults without the condition.

A study of adults with ADHD found that 19% met criteria for a mood disorder, including major depression, dysthymia, and bipolar disorders. Those with ADHD had similar rates of lifetime major depression but were more likely to meet criteria for bipolar disorder.

Women with ADHD were found to have higher rates of anxiety disorders, and pregnancy complicated or complicated by an anxious temperament is twice as common in women with ADHD than in women without the condition.

In addition to their own psychological needs and needs for support as a spouse or other family member, the lives of children of someone suffering from ADHD can suffer from this condition. National surveys found that about one in three children with ADHD will continue to have symptoms as an adult.

People with ADHD have a high incidence of accidents, with injuries ranging up to ten times higher than those without ADHD. Anywhere from 20-30% of adults with ADHD are injured in automobile accidents each year.

ADHD And Iq/Eq

People with ADHD tend to have a much lower or much higher IQ than the general population, with a correlation of -.66 between the two. This is likely because people with ADHD often have difficulty on tasks which require concentration and focus. Anyone diagnosed with ADHD has an IQ that falls anywhere from 55-145 on average, whereas the typical IQ for someone without ADHD falls from 90-110. This means that people with ADHD are about 2 ½ times more likely to have a below-average IQ than the population as a whole, and 4 ½ times more likely to have an above-average IQ.

"ADHD is characterized by impairment in behavioral inhibition, sustained attention and vigilance, working memory and executive functions". Impairment in these functions can often result in lower IQ for those with ADHD compared to those without. This is due to the fact that ADHD symptoms fall under the category of "developmental disorders" which are defined as "characterized by functional deficits in at least two domains: social interaction; communication; independent living skills; academic learning or motivation; or self-help skills. The term 'developmental disorders' includes all autism spectrum disorders, specific language impairment (SLI) and intellectual disability (ID)." This means that having symptoms of ADHD can lower IQ even in those who don't have the disorder.

"A study published in Child Brain Development reported that the children with ADHD failed to reach their full cognitive potential by age four (Swift et al., 2009), and a review paper on the topic by Ortega found a correlation between full-scale IQ and habitual application of methylphenidate or amphetamine but not a relation between dosage and IQ in children with ADHD. (Ortega, 2011)" This means that even children who are on medication for ADHD can still have lower IQ. This is most likely because the prefrontal cortex as well as the rest of the brain are developing longer than usual in children with ADHD.

"A study published in Journal of Child Psychology and Psychiatry found that kids between 7 and 9 years old with ADHD made less progress at reading than non-ADHD children, despite being just as able when they started school (Skirbekk et al., 2006)" This supports what was mentioned above. Even when on medication and other treatment methods for ADHD, it's difficult to make up lost ground in a child's development which could result in a lower IQ level.

With ADHD, there is a high risk for you to have an IQ that is lower than the norm. They can also have excellent memory skills and reasoning abilities despite their poor attention span. However, there are many educational resources available specifically designed to help you succeed academically with ADHD.

Ever wonder why some people are naturally so smart? Why do they seem to know everything at an early age? Well, it turns out that we all start off smarter than society gives us credit for! Individuals who score highly on intelligence tests were actually chosen more often by their parents as children and received more attention from them. They also occurred to get more education and had greater access to learning tasks, such as piano and foreign languages. In fact, they had the same access to learning environments that parents gave preferential attention to, from a young age. This means that the smartest children usually start with a higher IQ and have a better chance of continuing on with good mental processing skills throughout their lives. Some of this can be attributed to genetics because the chances of having a higher IQ are inherited by both twins and other family members (which is why identical twins have nearly identical IQ scores). However, this phenomenon happens even if only one child in the family has ADHD.

 The goal is not to shame them or make them feel bad about their condition. The reality is that ADHD causes many children to be all over the place mentally, and it can hurt their social skills at school and sometimes out in social situations. They may struggle with organization, forgetfulness and poor time management but they are usually good at things that require lots of creativity and memory skills like art, music and sports. However, these activities don't require academic skills so they may feel left out. The goal is to try and show your child that there are ways to harness their frustration and turn it into something positive.

It's simply a matter of breaking down the sides of their disorder and finding out what works for them. For instance, if you or your child seem to do well on tasks that use logic, like math and science, there's a good chance they will excel at problem solving. If you take a look at their learning capabilities, you can find out if they respond well to visual aids or auditory stimulation. For example, some people can learn more effectively when watching an instructor demonstrate something versus listening to them explain it verbally. Another big learning tip is to provide your child with a calm learning environment, ideally one that is free of distraction. This way they can focus their attention better and therefore sharpen their concentration abilities.

However, there are some important implications that should be examined. Since many children are diagnosed with ADHD as they progress in school, it can be a major roadblock to achieving their full potential. Many kids have been able to overcome this issue by getting an IEP or 504 plan through their local schools so that they may get the accommodations and resources they need in order to succeed academically. So if you think you might have ADHD but aren't sure what it means for your IQ, give your school a call!

After all, everyone deserves access to equal education.

ADHD and IQ are two of the most commonly-thought about mental health conditions that can have a large impact on someone's ability to function in their day-to-day life. Both are fairly prevalent, affecting hundreds of thousands of people worldwide. This will provide an overview of both ADHD and IQ, with an added focus on how to think about these conditions and make sense of them for yourself.

ADHD is what we commonly think of as a disorder of attention and memory. Those with ADHD have a very hard time with focusing, being able to resist all the distractions that life throws at us. They also tend to have trouble with concentration and attention span, and often get bored easily. This is why they are so impulsive, in an effort to keep themselves from getting bored. Their hyperactivity is also a manifestation of this boredom.

There is currently a genetic association between ADHD and lower-than-average IQ. There are two genes in particular that are associated with a smaller brain volume, which can be inferred to also mean fewer neurons, or less effective neurons. This means that people who have ADHD tend to have smaller brains.

This may explain why they have trouble focusing and concentrating, as the brain is simply not working at its full capacity. It is also possible that their brain is not working in the most efficient way. Is it just possible that ADHD explains away a genetic predisposition to low IQ as well as to ADHD? Just how bad are they for their brains?

Research on children with ADHD has found that both the severity of symptoms and the timing of development roughly follow advances in academic performance. This means that they tend to do much better when they are through the toughest parts of school, but often struggle when they get into higher-performing programs later on.

While there are different types of ADHD, there are two main points that seem to be present in all individuals with this condition. The first is a problem in the executive control system, which helps us to direct our attention and make decisions. The second is a lack of control over one's emotions.

Impulsivity seems to go hand-in-hand with ADHD and IQ. For instance, impulsivity has been shown to correlate with academic performance. A study of students found that those with higher levels of impulsivity tended to have lower IQs than those without impulsivity ($p=0.005$).

The emotional control system is also part of the executive control system and has been shown to be an important part of ADHD. One study on teenagers found that those who were impulsive had significantly lower IQs than those without impulsivity ($p=0.001$).

ADHD and EQ

Some people are great at multitasking or being flexible. They bounce from one thing to the next and can balance their priorities with ease. But for others, this is not the case - they quickly become overwhelmed, feel like they have little control over what they're doing, and struggle to stay focused on one task. These individuals may be described as having "Attention Deficit Hyperactivity Disorder," but recent research has shown that many people who do not have ADHD may also suffer from a lower EQ (Emotional Quotient) than those who do. In these cases, it's not the lack of focus that would be considered as "disorder," but rather the inability to process emotions in a healthy way.

Emotional Intelligence

"EQ" may be defined as a person's ability to recognize emotions in others and his or her own emotions, think and respond to other people's feelings, use emotional information to make good decisions and deal with criticism. It is commonly measured by tests that ask about how well a person understands himself or herself; how well one can manage his or her own feelings; and how well he or she interacts with others. The EQ scale ranges from 0 to 1, where higher numbers indicate better EQ.

Emotional Intelligence or EQ concept was first described in 1995, by two psychologists at the University of New Hampshire. Since then, the topic has received a lot of attention; however, controversy exists over how to define it and whether it is truly distinct from IQ (Intelligence Quotient). According to some definitions, EQ is simply another term for social intelligence, emotional self-awareness or social competence.

A low emotional intelligence (low EQ) can have a big effect on an individual's life. It can make it hard to respond in positive ways to things like criticism or stress and may cause difficulties with co-workers at work or friends socially. Studies have shown that low EQ individuals may also be less satisfied with their lives and jobs and may also have marital problems. Having low EQ has even been linked to being a bad parent!

Pathophysiology

Women with attention-deficit/hyperactivity disorder often have the stereotype of being overly emotional and easily distracted, but the truth is that there are a variety of symptoms that need to be addressed in order to provide treatment. Pathophysiology of Women with ADHD starts by providing an overview of what women with ADHD experience. It then proceeds to discuss their specific symptoms in further detail, including whether they are related to their physical or psychological health. The article concludes by discussing how best physicians can approach these unique concerns when deciding on a treatment plan for patients. "Pathophysiology of Women with ADHD" by Svetlana K. Kvalsvig argues that women experience a different array of symptoms than what is typically associated with ADHD, and they may even manifest new symptoms not previously observed in men with the disorder.

Women have a higher chance than men to seek medical attention for another condition instead of being diagnosed with ADHD, which is why this study states that it "is important to pay specific attention to the presence or absence of symptoms as well as their severity." This article also states that because many women are not diagnosed until later in life, it is important for physicians to begin by asking patients about their history during childhood and adolescence, as well as about any current concerns.

It is estimated that by adulthood, about 80 percent of individuals with ADHD are diagnosed, but only about 50 percent of children get treatment. Adults may be more hesitant to receive an ADHD diagnosis because they fear the social stigma of having a psychiatric disorder. However, these women may experience significant impairment in multiple facets of their lives that are not typical for those who have ADHD.

To address the unique symptomology and characteristics that women with ADHD can experience, it is recommended that physicians take an integrated approach to care. This includes assessing any risks for medical complications as well as psychological issues such as depression or anxiety. It is also recommending that physicians conduct a thorough physical examination of the patient in order to identify any possible endocrine issues, gastrointestinal problems, or hormonal irregularities.

Although many women with ADHD are mislabeled as having mood disorders, there are clear differences between the two. This suggests that men with bipolar disorder and women with ADHD may share symptoms such as distractibility and impulsivity, but both disorders have different triggers and "are associated with distinctive patterns of comorbidity and treatment response." For women with ADHD, the possibility of a bipolar disorder is still greater, as they are diagnosed more frequently than men with bipolar disorder. After a mental health evaluation and medical assessment, physicians will be able to determine the best course of treatment for patients.

Women face a few unique issues when it comes to developing an effective treatment plan for ADHD. The article states that both WesternMedicalPsychiatry and Chinese medicine are highly concerned with physical symptoms, and both disciplines use different diagnosis methods to identify whether or not there is an imbalance of qi, blood, or phlegm in the body. The Western process identifies physical symptoms and aims to balance the patients' qi, or life force energy. Chinese medicine focuses on identifying emotional imbalances and uses treatments such as herbal remedies or acupuncture to rebalance the patient's blood vitality.

Because of these differences in diagnosis techniques, it is difficult for Western practitioners to properly identify patients with ADHD who may have causes in Chinese medicine. A woman's menstrual cycle is very important during a physical examination, but it must also be considered that there are cultural reasons why women may not want to disclose this important information. This suggests that in order to properly diagnose women with ADHD, physicians need to consider methods that may be more sensitive and considerate of their patients' cultural backgrounds and preferences.

Although the symptoms experienced by women with ADHD are different from men, the disorder can still affect a woman's life equally as severely. Although it is estimated that half of those who have ADHD are diagnosed by adulthood, there are still many women who seek treatment after being misdiagnosed with other conditions. This provides an important framework for physicians that will help them determine when they should ask about a patient's history regarding ADHD, and how best to approach treatment for each woman with the disorder.

Stereotypes about hyperactivity in females tend to cause diagnosis delays, one study found that only 18% of females sought out help within three years after experiencing symptoms. The lack of formal diagnosis can seriously impact these individuals' lives not only academically but also socially and emotionally as well. Studies have shown that patients who are properly diagnosed and treated show significant improvements in every aspect of their lives.

Diagnosis

The Diagnostic and Statistical Manual (DSM) for the American Psychological Association (APA) asserts that your husband may have ADHD if he has experienced six or more of the following symptoms regularly for at least the past six month.

Inattention:

- Often fails to give close attention to the details or makes careless mistakes.
- Difficulty sustaining attention.
- Appears as though he is not listening when their spoken onto.
- Failed to follow through with instructions or tasks (not as a result of purposeful rebellion).
- Difficulties in getting or staying organizes
- Avoids dislikes, hesitates to engage in tasks that require sustained attention.
- Often loses or misplaces things
- Easily distracted
- Frequent forgetfulness
- Hyperactivity:
- Frequent fidgeting or squirming.
- Excessive physical activity and self-report feeling being restless
- Difficulties engaging on leisure activity quiet.
- Appears to be driven by an internal motor that seems never to stop running.

These symptoms must have been present in the individuals before the age of twelve. They must also be present in two or more settings (e.g., work and home). Individuals must be experiencing significant impairment in their ability to function at a developmentally appropriate level. Individuals who demonstrate at least six of the symptoms for both inattention AND hyperactivity qualify for the diagnosis of ADHD.

Dr. Edward Hallowell's book, driven to Distraction, describes a few other telltale signs that can further clarify whether the individual might have ADHD. However, these signs serve as just that—signs. A few of these symptoms might be a problem, but it does not necessarily mean that the individual has the real disorder.

According to Dr. Hallowell, anyone exhibiting at least 12 of the following characteristics since childhood, where the characteristics are not associated with any other psychological or medical condition, should consider being evaluated for ADHD:

- A persistent sense of underachievement, of not meeting one's goals (regardless of how much one has actually accomplished)
- Difficulty getting and/or staying organized
- Chronic procrastination or trouble initiating tasks
- Tendency to take on many projects simultaneously with trouble following through
- Lack of a verbal "filter"; the tendency to say what comes to mind without necessarily considering the timing or appropriateness of the remark
- Frequently in search of increasing levels of stimulation
- An intolerance of boredom
- Easily distractible; trouble focus attentions tendency the tune out or drift away in the middle of a page and conversation, often coupled with an inability to focus at times
- Often creative, intuitive, highly intelligent, but slightly eccentric
- Lack of conformity and/or following "proper" procedure when pursuing goals
- Impatience; low tolerance for frustration
- Impulsivity, either verbally or inaction (i.e., impulsively spending money or being hot-tempered)
- Frequently changing plans, enacting new schemes or career plans
- A persistent tendency to worry needlessly; scanning the horizons look for something to worry about alternative with the attention to or disregard for actual dangers
- A sense of insecurity
- Mood swings, especially when not currently engaged with a person or project
- Physical or cognitive restlessness
- A tendency toward addictive behavior
- Chronic problems with self-esteem
- Inaccurate self-observation; lack of personal insight

- Family history of ADHD, manic-depressive illness, depression, substance abuse, or other disorders of impulse control or mood

Many of these signs overlap with the DSM diagnostic criteria. However, there are others that do not. Some of them may be more indicative of another mental illness, so it is important to identify the primary problem. According to the 2007 study in Primary Care: Clinics in Office Practice, childhood ADHD symptoms often evolve into the following adult symptoms:

- Procrastination;
- Indecision, difficulty recalling and organize details requires in a task.
- Poor time management and losing track of time.
- Avoiding tasks and jobs that require sustained attention
- Trouble initiating tasks
- Difficulty completing and following through on tasks
- Seeming inability to multitask
- Difficulty of shifting attention from one task to another

Although a diagnosis of ADHD may initially be shocking to you and your family, you can breathe a sigh of relief, knowing you finally have a medical explanation for your husband's difficult behavior. What's more, you can start to take steps to help manage the disorder and improve both your lives.

In the meantime, remember that a diagnosis of ADHD does not imply low intelligence. You don't have to speak louder or more slowly for your husband to understand you. In fact, most people with ADHD are highly intelligence. It's only that their intelligence gets tangled up inside their brain and needs to be smoothed out in order for them to function optimistically.

Testing

Many psychological conditions can be detected by a blood test or brain scan. Some disorders are so distinct that there can be only one explanation for them. Unfortunately, this is not the case with ADHD. In fact, it can be difficult to make a definitive diagnosis for this disorder because there is no single test with the confident to diagnoses of disorder. Only a license and trained mental health professional can administer the current panel of evaluations to properly diagnose ADHD. Be wary of online quizzes claiming to diagnose ADHD quickly or for free. There is no quick diagnosis, just as there is no quick fix to treat it. Since the diagnosis can be difficult and carries a life sentence, it is imperative that the testing be done carefully and completely. Invest time and money necessary to get the correct diagnosis the first time and work only with mental health professionals with whom you feel comfortable.

A qualified professional should conduct a series of evaluations to provide an official diagnosis. At the Sachs Center, we employ three different methods of testing to arrive at a diagnosis. Checklists are also employed that are tested and researched by universities. An example is the Adult ADHD Self-Report Scale-V1.1 (ASRS-V1.1). Second, the client completes a computer exercise to uncover deficits in visual and auditory attention span symptoms of ADHD. We use and recommend the IVA+Plus, created by Brain Train. The IVA+Plus and other computer-based performance tests provide objective data regarding a person's ability to concentrate and to avoid making impulsive errors. Lastly, the client completes a battery of several short tests to assess working memory, processing speed, and executive functioning.

While each test alone cannot assess for ADHD, together, they provide a clearer picture of the individual's strengths and weaknesses and help the clinician come to an accurate diagnosis.

Note: Some clinics recommend an expensive, eight-hour neuropsychological assessment to determine a diagnosis of ADHD. This is generally not necessary unless there is other serious co-occurring mental health or neurological issues. Attention-shortfall/hyperactivity issue (AD/HD or ADHD)

ADHD is the turmoil of the brain and conduct. It influences around 3 to 5% of children. The side effects start before seven years old. Worldwide commonness for children is roughly 5%, with wide changeability subject to look into philosophies used in examines. Consideration Deficit Hyperactivity Disorder and ADHD is one of the most widely recognized mental issues create in children Children with ADHD have impeded working in numerous settings including home, school, and involved with peers. On the off chance that untreated, the confusion can have long haul antagonistic impacts into puberty and adulthood.

Indications/Symptoms: The most widely recognized indications of ADHD are:

Rashness: acting before considering outcomes, hopping starting with one movement then onto the next, disorder, inclination to intrude on other people groups' discussions

Hyperactivity: fretfulness, frequently described by a failure to sit as yet, squirming, squirminess, jumping on things, eager rest.

Absentmindedness: effectively diverted, staring off into space, not completing work, trouble tuning in.

Subtypes: ADHD has three subtypes:

Dominatingly hyperactive-imprudent

Most side effects (at least six) are in the hyperactivity-impulsivity classifications. Less than six side effects of heedlessness are available, in spite of the fact that obliviousness may, in any case, be available somewhat.

Transcendently inattentive

Most of the manifestations (at least six) are in the mindlessness classification, and less than six side effects of hyperactivity-impulsivity are available, despite the fact that hyperactivity-impulsivity may, in any case, be available somewhat.

Children with this subtype are more averse to carry on or experience issues coexisting with other children. They may sit unobtrusively, yet they are not focusing on what they are doing. Subsequently, the kid might be neglected, and guardians and educators may not see that the person in question has ADHD.

Joined hyperactive-rash and inattentive

At least six indications of obliviousness and at least six side effects of hyperactivity-impulsivity are available. Most children have the joined kind of ADHD.

Causes

A particular reason for ADHD isn't known. There are, in any case, various variables that may add to ADHD, including hereditary qualities, diet, and social and physical situations.

Hereditary factors

Studies demonstrate that the confusion is exceptionally heritable and that hereditary quality are a factor in about 75% of ADHD cases. Hyperactivity, likewise, is by all accounts basically a hereditary condition anyway, and different causes do have an impact.

Specialists accept that a vastly larger part of ADHD cases emerges from a blend of different qualities, a significant number of which influence dopamine (a compound in the brain) transporters. The wide determination of targets shows that ADHD doesn't pursue the conventional model of a "hereditary malady" and ought to hence be seen as unpredictable cooperation among hereditary and ecological variables.

Ecological factors

Natural variables involved incorporating liquor and tobacco smoke introduction during pregnancy and ecological presentation to lead in early life.

What You Should Know and Understand About Medications

Many people have an anti-medication perspective. When they hear that one of the main types of stimulants is a methamphetamine molecule, the association with 'street meth' is understandable and evokes visions of being drug dependent. The fundamental differences lie in dose (milligrams vs. grams with methamphetamine abuse) and the fact that the molecule found in medications is a pharmacological standard. The irony is that treating ADD/ADHD can reduce the likelihood of chemical dependency problems with girls and bring it to a point where it is on a par with non-ADD males.

People also worry about not feeling like themselves and that they will be emotionally blunted. This is a marker that suggests the person is on the wrong class of medications. A skilled provider should ask about this nuance of a response. Some of my therapy clients have made the suggestion that 'insight' is a possible side effect. Many others note profound changes in their sense of being in the world.

Stimulants represent the first line of treatment for people with ADD/ADHD. There are also non-stimulant and antidepressant preparations in current use. When compared to the effectiveness of stimulants, these are second-tier choices.

A variety of neurotransmitters are responsible for higher brain functions. They are the signalers for a wide variety of emotional states. They are implicated in an array of psychiatric illnesses. The medications are used to address these functions by regulating the availability of an assortment of neurotransmitters. They play a role in decision-making, control of our impulses, motor integration, and memory. While an in-depth discussion of neurotransmitter activity is beyond the scope of this book, it stimulates affect neurotransmitter activity in the brain leading to changes in both brain physiology and activity (1).

There are two types or classes of stimulants available. They are the methylphenidates (MPH) and the methamphetamine salts (MAS). They both affected the same parts of the brain, albeit with slightly different biochemical pathways. What determines which class of medication is better for an individual is a matter of both toleration and response? Poor reactions to medications are often due to the fact they have not been on the right medication. Generally, switching the class of medication will address problems with toleration. There are people who don't tolerate either class of stimulants. It happens, but fortunately, lack of toleration is an infrequent occurrence.

Strattera (atomoxetine) is a non-stimulant preparation for the treatment of ADD/ADHD. It provides 24-hour coverage with a single daily dose. It takes six to eight weeks to evaluate response as contrasted to the stimulants, where you figure out the best class and best dose in several weeks.

Treatment

Medications for adult ADHD affect the neurotransmitters in your brain responsible for attention and motivation. While stimulant drugs have long been considered the first line of defense in treating the disorder and are still widely regarded as the most effective, they are by no means the only type of medication. Many non-stimulant drugs, including antidepressants, anticonvulsants, waking agents, and even estrogen, have proven beneficial. Strattera, a relatively new non-stimulant drug that's the only medication approved by the FDA specifically for adult ADHD, shows great promise in treating the disorder.

National Institutes of Health Landmark Study

Adult ADHD and depression often go hand-in-hand, and a multi-treatment approach often works best to alleviate symptoms of the disorder. A 2006 landmark study funded by the NIH showed that using various antidepressants may also help relieve depression in adults.

One out of three people suffering from chronic depression found relief from symptoms after adding a second medication in the study. One in four became symptom-free after switching to a different antidepressant. The medications included sertraline (Zoloft), bupropion-SR (Wellbutrin), and venlafaxine-XR (Effexor), three different types of antidepressants.

Essential

To date, no psychostimulants routinely prescribed for adult ADHD have been approved by the FDA specifically for the treatment of the disorder. For the reason these drugs are often prescribed "off label," or used for reasons other than the standard prescribed use.

The research also showed that if your first treatment or medication isn't successful, the best course of action is to work with your physician to change or add another medication until you find a combination that works. Studies have shown that stimulant medication is a safe, long-term solution for adult ADHD.

Challenges in Medicating Adults with ADHD

Research funded by NIMH indicates that medication is most effective when a physician routinely monitors treatment. Adults may also benefit from a change in dose or schedule. Long-acting medications are taken once a day, rather than in multiple doses, seem to work best for most adults.

Short-duration stimulants may wear off quickly. Since many adult patients have forgetfulness, taking multiple doses during the day can leave them unprotected if they forget to take the second and third doses. Adults who are tempted to take stimulants at night to help them calm down may wind up feeling so relaxed they can't focus on household chores, homework, completing projects for work, paying bills, or even driving.

The Problem with Substance Abuse

Research shows that 60 to 80 percent adults with ADHD experience a dramatic reduction of symptoms after taking stimulant drugs. While using stimulants to treat adult ADHD may seem paradoxical, studies show mild stimulants have a dramatic calming effect on the brains and nerves of adults with ADHD and also reduce the incidence of substance abuse among treated adults.

However, because many adults with ADHD have a history of substance abuse, and because stimulant drugs are scheduling II controlled substances, some believe there's a chance they may be tempted to use their ADHD medication for recreational purposes.

Fact

Research shows that adults with ADHD being treated with stimulants have a lower incidence of substance abuse than other adults and are also less likely to self-medicate with illegal substances than adults with undiagnosed adult ADHD. Recent studies showed that most adults taking Ritalin lower their dose of stimulants across time rather than increasing the dose.

The people with a recent history of substance use but no current use deciding to use stimulant medication should be dealt with on a case-by-case basis. Specific extended-release preparations are less likely to be abused. One example is Concerta, which can't be crushed and used other than as prescribed orally.

In general, medications with a gradual onset of effect and long duration of effect are likely to work most smoothly, avoiding emotional ups and downs. These are also the best formulations for people with a history of substance abuse because they avoid the "hit" and "buzz" of recreational stimulants.

Viviane, a new medication for adult ADHD, is a "pro-drug." After you ingest the medication, the body converts it to a stimulant, which lessens the potential for abuse.

Differences in Treating Children and Adults

While many of the medications are the same as those used for children and adolescents, there are several general differences to consider. Although adults are generally larger than children, they may need less medication per pound of bodyweight because the drug may remain in their system longer if they don't have healthy liver and kidney function.

In addition, adults are more likely to be taking medications for other conditions, some of which may interact with ADHD drugs and interfere with their potency. Many medications taken by adults for coexisting conditions may also cause lethargy, anxiety, and insomnia or exacerbate adult ADHD symptoms.

The Practice of Polypharmacy

Polypharmacy, or prescribing several psychiatric medications simultaneously, is often used to treat coexisting conditions in adults with ADHD. For instance, if an adult has ADHD and clinical anxiety, she may need to take medication for both conditions. If done correctly, polypharmacy can result in a simultaneous reduction of symptoms for both conditions. But if medications are prescribed without considering their various side effects, a patient could suffer severe medical consequences or even experience an increase in symptoms.

Most Commonly Prescribed

Drugs to Treat Adult ADHD

Over the past fifteen years, the medication options for treating adult ADHD have greatly expanded. Today, the most popular medications for treating the disease include stimulant drugs and a wide variety of non-stimulant drugs in various drug categories.

Despite the growing number of medication options, stimulant medications, including methylphenidate (such as Ritalin) and dextroamphetamine compounds (Dextrostat, Dexedrine Spansules, and Adderall), remain the most commonly prescribed drugs for adult ADHD.

Stimulant medications like Ritalin and Adderall remain the most frequently prescribed drugs, but they are no longer the only line of defense for adults with ADHD. Other medications that are sometimes prescribed off-label for adult ADHD include TCAs such as Elavil.

Medications prescribed for co-morbid conditions include serotonin selective reuptake inhibitors, such as Prozac and Zoloft, and mood stabilizers. Although the FDA has approved no antidepressants for treating adult ADHD, they are often prescribed off-label to alleviate its symptoms.

In 2002, the non-stimulant drug Strattera became the first medication approved by the FDA to treat ADHD in adults. Strattera is not a Class II stimulant, so there is also no abuse potential.

Things to Remember If You're Considering Medication

Drug treatment for adult ADHD requires that you maintain an open line of communication with your physician to ensure you are taking the right drug at the correct dose. This can be vital if you suffer adverse side effects and need to take corrective measures or if a drug stop working for you.

Medications are not magic bullets or cures but part of an overall treatment approach. Because the first medication you try may not be the drug that offers you the most benefits, it's essential to pay attention to how medications affect your symptoms and what side effects occur.

Medication for adult ADHD can help relieve symptoms. Still, it should not be regarded as a substitute for mastering strategies and healthy lifestyle habits or the many types of therapies that could help you better cope daily with the symptoms and challenges presented by the disorder.

Remember to be patient; you and your doctor may need to experiment with various medications before finding the medication, amount, and dosing schedule that work best for you.

The Role of Clinical Trials

Clinical trials are done to isolate distinct symptoms of ADHD in adults and develop new medications and treatments.

However, more clinical trials are needed to determine if adult ADHD medications alleviate symptoms and lead to permanent improvements in executive functions like planning, organizing, and prioritizing.

Focus on Stimulant Drugs

Stimulants come in a variety of forms and brands. Stimulant medications are considered safe when taken under medical supervision. Used as prescribed, they do not make adults with ADHD feel high.

Although the majority—60 to 80 percent—of adults with ADHD enjoy a dramatic decrease in symptoms when taking medication, some only receive a small benefit while others reap none at all.

Others suffer from side effects that are so severe that they must go off the drugs.

How Stimulants Work in the Brain

Stimulant medications are believed to directly affect the brain neurotransmitters dopamine and norepinephrine, responsible for transmitting messages between different parts of the brain.

Dopamine controls the power of the signals coming into your brain and regulates areas of the brain that control filtering and screening. Norepinephrine controls your level of alertness, clarity, and wakefulness. Both neurotransmitters impact motivation and are also believed to affect attention and behavioral symptoms, although how these works remain unknown.

Alert

Seventy-five percent of adults with ADHD also have coexisting conditions. Generic stimulants are usually inexpensive, although many longer-acting stimulants can be pretty expensive if your insurance doesn't cover medication costs.

Forms of Stimulant Medication

Stimulant medications come in pills, capsules, liquids, and skin patches. Some the medications also come in short-acting, long-acting, or extended-release varieties. The active ingredient is the same in each of these varieties, but it is released differently in the body.

Long-acting or extended-release forms ("ER" or "XR") often work best for adults who need continuous relief during daytime and evening hours and who may be too forgetful or distracted to remember to take second and third doses. They are also prescribed people for whom substance abuse is a concern.

The Half-Life of Medication

The half-life of a drug refers to the amount of time it takes a drug to reach 50 percent of its peak effectiveness after you take a dose.

The longer the half-life of a drug, the longer it takes for the drug to reach its full effect, and the more critical it is to take it on time to maintain a steady level of medication in your bloodstream.

Neglecting to take drugs with a short half-life on time may result in a condition called discontinuation syndrome. Symptoms include irritability, insomnia, dizziness, light-headedness, and flu-like symptoms and may persist for weeks.

Commonly Prescribed Stimulants

There are many different kinds of stimulant drugs your physician may prescribe. Although they all work similarly, they differ in how quickly they begin to work, how extended 1they remain in your bloodstream, the degree of relief they provide, and their side effects. Through trial-and-error, you and your physician will be able to determine which medication(s) work best for you.

7 Practical Strategies for Improving Your Life

Hearing news about ADHD is not astounding nowadays because there are many such instances of the condition, which have been accounted for. Truth be told, when you discover a news article on ADHD on the web, or a child with ADHD is featured on a TV program, you would locate these conventional. What is astounding about the condition, however, is that adults can sit with it. Yes, there is without a doubt adult ADHD case accounted for. Besides, there are very many! In America alone there is more than 12 million instances of ADHD in adults, which have been accounted for.

In any case, about diagnosing the condition in adults, the procedure is more troublesome when contrasted with that of diagnosing children. There is very little research done on adults with ADHD, which adds to this trouble. Another cause for this trouble is how symptoms of ADHD are shown in children, which are unique compared to adults. Subsequently, you cannot generally look at the conditions solidly by any means. The subject of hereditary inclinations has also not been set up in adults with ADHD yet. in the off chance that you speculate you could have ADHD as an adult, the wise things to do here is to have yourself checked by your doctor. Your past conduct and medicinal history will be assessed entirely.

Medicinal and physical exams will likewise be direct to decide any probable causes that may have set off the onset of ADHD symptoms.

The symptoms of ADHD in adults can be relative. Much like ADHD cases in children, each must be treated as impartially as could be expected under the circumstances. Still, there are general symptoms that are generally found in adult patients. The following are a portion of the symptoms to look out for when considering the condition.

Sorting out exercises and finishing errands can be exceptionally hard to do if you are living with ADHD. These abilities are required in any given occupation. Being inadequate in these aptitudes can be exceptionally disturbing for any expert. Adults distressed with ADHD frequently lose things when they are amidst doing assignments and exercises. It is primarily due to how the individual is easily distracted by any jolt that can snatch their attention.

For more data, you can investigate the DSM, or the Diagnostic and Statistical Manual of Mental Disorders produced and created by the American Psychiatric Association or the APA. The DSM contains all the found symptoms of adult ADHD.

From the minute that they are awake, they have feelings that they should have been up hours before to ensure that everything is completed; the adult ADHD sufferer is never fulfilled.

On the other side, there will be different days when nothing, literally nothing, fits appropriately, and a similar individual will spend the entire day in a foggy, dumbfounded state, always mindful of the things that they ought to do, yet never thoroughly having the vitality or excitement to handle the occupations close.

They subsequently end an inadmissible day feeling grim, dormant, befuddled, and for the most part, inconsistent with the world.

Neither of these situations is an essential piece of being an adult ADHD sufferer!

On the off chance that you can see yourself in this photo, and then you should comprehend there are many things where you can do to begin breaking out of this to some degree inconsequential. Yet! Overall are a horrible circle.

Here are seven basic tips or abilities that you can begin to apply to your consistent life to attempt to enhance things

1. Attempt to relax.

Adult ADHD sufferers are quite often inclined to move and act a great deal more rapidly than other individuals. To such an extent, truth told, that frequently, they never appear to complete one employment proceeding onward to the following. Attempt to make a stride once again from life occasionally and try to back off. Take a gander at everyone around you and attempt to go at his or her speed instead of the one that your ordinary senses are pushing you towards.

2. Set aside a few minutes for you.

Numerous adult ADHD sufferers tend to put every other person in front of themselves or themselves in the line. At the same time, this is probably an excellent quality; attempt to put yourself forward for a touch of uncommon treatment now and again as well!

3. Know yourself and your condition.

ADHD and the other related types of ADD will unexpectedly influence each unique sufferer. Attempt to see precisely how your condition influences you as an individual, and therefore, give yourself more shot at managing your condition and conditions.

4. Know your qualities and work with them.

Regardless of whether you are an adult ADHD sufferer or not, each person has qualities and shortcomings, and you are no exemption to run the show. Know your solid focuses, what you are great at, concentrate on them, and attempt to arrange your day utilizing these qualities. This will help you abstain from getting into the negative winding of continually moving yet never really going anywhere

5. Remain upbeat and positive about your life

If you are always negative and cynical, then life will never be something you can appreciate or get the most out of. Therefore, notwithstanding when things are entirely and going great truly, by the by, you will dependably be searching for the negative side. Think emphatically and do all that you can to be idealistic every single day.

6. Arrange everything that it is conceivable to arrange.

Most adult ADHD sufferers are not normally great at arranging their day, or without a doubt, their lives. Nevertheless, by arranging legitimately and setting up practical objectives and destinations, you can start to consider yourself more effective than you may have beforehand accepted. Dealing with your time along these lines will help back you off, and in this manner, you will tend to accomplish a horrendous part more than you already oversaw.

7. Move yourself.

Attempt new things at whatever point you can and venture out of your usual range of familiarity into the obscure. By doing this, you get away from the murmur drum routine into which it is very simple for the adult ADHD-influenced individual to fall, and this escape will an end in itself help to revive your general get-up-and-go and eagerness forever. Try not to utilize your condition as a reason to remain in your usual range of familiarity, since it is this safe place that anxieties the normal adult ADHD sufferer out! Experiment as regularly would be prudent because a change truly IS on a par with rest, the same amount for an adult ADHD-influenced individual as it is for any other individual.

Adults With ADHD: Facing the Day with a Plan

Adults who suffer from ADHD tend to find details difficult to absorb. They do have those clear goals in their heads, but it is difficult to wait for them to be achieved. Sadly, this kind of attitude that will get the person overwhelmed whenever they are starting with a new project. They can clearly see the result but have no idea the steps to make it happen.

This is the same with the little tasks that need to be done every day. Those who suffer from ADHD may begin the day with clear objectives that need to be reached but are unable to organize themselves to get started on them. This can cause feelings of stress and guilt. This also leads to generally feeling low in their abilities, and then the idea of getting things done seems a long way off.

How to Stop This from Happening?

To begin with, adults should start the day by sitting down and planning their routine. The easy way to apply this is to make sure these three steps are following.

Step 1 – Decide the Exact Time of Morning the Plan Should Be Written

Decide first which time of day the plan/daily schedule is written. It will take about 15 minutes or less to write everything down. A specific time could be decided, such as 8.15 am. On the other hand, it could be something like 'right after breakfast.' Sometimes, it is good to get into the habit of writing out a plan for the next day just before you go to bed.

Writing out the plan the night before is a great option for those with ADHD. This is usually the time when the greatest signs of alertness happen.

Step 2 – Review the List

When you complete any of the tasks listed, cross it off. If you think of another task that needs to be done, add it to the list. This should help you feel that progress is being made and, in turn, make you feel better about yourself.

Step 3 - Use a Calendar

Once you have got used to making daily plans, the next step is to make a list of tasks that need to be taken care of later. This is where the use of a calendar comes in. Any appointments, meetings, visits, etc., that will be happening later that month or later that year should be noted on the calendar under the correct date. This will also act as a handy reminder when it comes to writing your daily task list as you can look at your calendar and see if anything is outstanding that needs to be added.

These are simple things to do which will not take a great deal of time to put into action. If you get to feel organized, then you will get to feel better about yourself.

I'd like to talk to you as if you were sitting in my office. There are certain issues and scenarios that tend to come up repeatedly for teens with ADHD, and while you are all unique and have different problems, it's important to know that you aren't alone and there is most likely someone else who is going through whatever you are going through. I'm right here, so let's go through it together.

Q: Today was my third day late to first-period English. I have been having a hard time with the homework, and if I show up late, I avoid having to turn in the assignment I didn't do. If I'm late one more time, I receive detention, and my parents get called. My parents and my teacher are already on my case for not keeping up with my homework. What should I do?

A: It sounds like things are piling up at school, and you are feeling pretty overwhelmed. Tempting as it may be to hide this from your parents and your teacher, you need to sit down with them and be honest about what is currently giving you difficulty. When you feel overwhelmed it can seem as though everything is crashing down around you. But a good way to avoid feeling like this is to pinpoint specific problems that you may be able to work on.

Try this: Write down specifically what is hard about getting your English homework done. Here are some questions/prompts that may help you:

Are you struggling with the concepts? If so, you may need to speak to your teacher about extra help after class or working with a tutor.

Are you having a hard time focusing? In this is the case, you may want to talk to your parents about what can be done to help, and don't forget to check out the exercises here and here.

Are you having a hard time writing or getting your ideas onto paper? Try using a mind map (see here) or working with a writing tutor.

Once you have your answer, sit down with your parents and let them know what is going on. Reach out to your teacher and share your concerns. Ask your parents and teacher to help you develop a plan to get back on track.

Q: Since I started high school, my supposed best friend started hanging out with some new friends. She doesn't invite me out when she is with them, and recently, she doesn't even say hi to me in the hallway. I feel really hurt and rejected.

A: It's really painful when someone you care about seems to move on without you. Feeling hurt and rejected is completely normal. It's importance to make sure that you have someone to talk to. Here are some things to remember:

High school is a time of transition and experimentation. Your friend may be trying out a new group of friends, and she may not intentionally be ignoring you but may just be rather swept up in the excitement. Consider to tell her about how you feel during a quiet moment alone with her.

Reevaluate your support network. While no one likes feeling left in the dust, you can make some changes to help lessen the pain. Is there a new activity you can join? Are there other friends you can spend more time with?

Think of your friends as a bank account. You should both be making deposits and withdrawals to keep your friendship healthy. If it feels like a friendship is draining, you and only makes you feel negative feelings. May be this is the time to reevaluate your investment in it.

Q: My parents are mad at me for constantly lying to them. Last night, I promised them I would clean up my room, but I didn't, and when they asked what I got on my Latin test, I told them I got an A when I really got a D. My mom says my first instinct is to lie and I think deep down she is right. Sometimes I make up lies to cover up other lies that I've told them. Why do I do this?

A: It can be tempting to tell people (especially your parents) what they want to hear, even if it's not the truth. No one wants to give bad or disappointing news or admit to our own shortcomings. The problem with lying is that it's not a solution to a problem and lying will only make things worse.

Here some questions to help you understand, why you may be avoiding the truth.

- •Are you worried about getting criticism or disappointing someone?
- •Will telling the truth get you into trouble?
- •Are you avoiding something you are having difficulty with (such as a long-term project that you don't know how to start or studying for a test you don't feel hopeful about)?
- •Do you feel like your parents' expectations are too high for you?

By paying more attention to the worries or concerns that lead you to lie about something, it may help you realize why you resort to bending the truth. Work on solving those problems, and eventually, you will feel more comfortable speaking the truth.

Being ADHD

As ADHD grows in prevalence, so does the stigma surround it. Many think it means students are lazy or stupid. Even some adults think they can trick a doctor into giving them a diagnosis so they can get stimulants for studying and become better at work. ADHD is frustrating – but not as difficult as being misunderstood. The following discusses the pros and cons of having ADHD: from being hyperactive to staying at home all day, from being unable to focus to loving anything new and exciting, from quickly getting bored in school to excelling with difficult tasks, from never finishing homework assignments to living life on the high-octane side without even trying.

Hyperactivity

The most obvious pro of having ADHD is that there is a lot of energy to do things. Many ADHD students are very social and popular. They are the leaders in clubs and other extracurricular activities such as sports, music, and drama. They may be the class clowns, but they also raise group morale with their enthusiasm.

Many people like working out at the gym because it makes them feel good about themselves to get stronger and look better. ADHD students can have this same experience by taking advantage of their energy to make their lives more productive, fun, and enjoyable.

Attention Deficit Hyperactivity Disorder, or ADHD, is a neurobiological condition that makes it difficult for people to pay attention and learn new information – two things it is necessary in life. There are many ways to be good at both paying attention and learning. Some people might have an easier time than others with these issues but no one is truly "bad" at them. Students with ADHD can use their hyperactivity to their advantage by choosing activities that will help them become better learners and more successful students overall.

Advantages of ADHD

Because people with ADHD seem to be able to accomplish more than others it makes sense that they might have certain advantages over other people who do not have this condition.

The Pros:

Being able to see more details at once.

Being able to hear more sounds at once.

Being able to respond to many situations quickly.

Being able to multitask better than others. With ADHD, there are many things going on in a person's brain all at the same time but individuals with this disorder are rarely distracted by extraneous thoughts or other things around them that keep them from focusing on what they need to do.

Being able to learn faster.

Being able to memorize information quicker. People with ADHD are often more aware of the words or numbers they are trying to remember. They focus on what they are supposed to have learned and they follow through on their studies and assignments quickly and efficiently. They do not get distracted by extraneous ideas or other thoughts.

Being able to work harder than other people when it comes to studying, sports and other creative pursuits.

- Having a mind that constantly needs stimulation

- Having a quick mental process that can think outside the box and solve problems quickly

- Being able to get lost in your own world and explore your imagination

The Cons

- The tendency for people with ADHD to be easily bored and need something new or a change of pace all the time

- Procrastination because you are easily distracted by other things when you should really focus on one task at a time, such as reading an article or finishing homework. This can cause school grades to drop.

- Lack of self-control in activities like watching TV, eating, or spending too much time on social media sites. - You might be missing important details in a lecture or social situations due to mental confusion.

- The inability to stay on task at work, school, or in relationships. You could lose out on learning opportunities or opportunities for friendship because you find it difficult to focus well when others are talking.

- The inability to follow through with plans and projects that you make. You jump from one idea to the next without finishing a project before moving onto another one.

- Can become easily overwhelmed when writing long essays, reading textbooks, completing tests, listening to lectures in school or lectures about complex topics like psychology or history.

- A person with ADHD might be easily distracted by people around you. They are also easily bored if they do not have many stimuli such as conversations or an interesting TV show to watch.

- People with ADHD can become negative, sarcastic, and impatient in social situations that require patience or understanding.

- People with ADHD often have a short attention span, especially when it comes to reading something lengthy like a book or study material at school; this makes it difficult for them to learn the material they read because their mind is so full of incoming information from other things that are happening around them.

- You might have a hard time reading social or emotional cues, such as seeing how someone is feeling; you might misread people's emotions and feel like you are being attacked if they are upset with you.

- Can become easily bored and distracted in your daily routine. The monotony of a regular life can be extremely difficult for someone with ADHD which makes it hard to complete regular tasks like homework, chores, or cleaning the house.

- You may find yourself making mistakes in schoolwork or at work over and over again simply because you didn't focus long enough to see how to complete the task correctly.

- Most people with ADHD have a lower self-esteem than their neurotypical counterparts. This is because of the low self-esteem that comes with constantly feeling frustrated with yourself because you can't complete what you need to get done. The other reasons for this are the feelings of inadequacy and frustration that can often arise in social situations.

- People with ADHD often have a hard time relaxing and enjoying leisure time activities because their mind is always going 100 miles a minute. Even when they are not doing anything, they have trouble being still and letting their mind slow down.

- This inability to relax and enjoy leisure time or spend time with loved ones can make it difficult for you in relationships as well as friendships because people without ADHD might become frustrated by your inability to slow down and do things at regular speed.

- Attention Deficit Disorder can often cause relationship issues with people you live with or family members because you are inclined to be more negative, impatient, and sarcastic than your family members might like.

- You might have a hard time understanding the emotions of others even if you aren't just being sarcastic or negative. This inability to read social cues or understand the emotions of others could lead to problems in romantic relationships because it is not only difficult for someone with ADHD to stay focused on one thing at a time, but it is also difficult for them to be patient and UNDERSTAND what their partner needs in a relationship.

- The inability to focus and the need for constant stimulation can lead to you having a negative outlook on life. You might think that there is nothing good in life or that everything sucks and that you're going to have a terrible day, even though it might be the opposite.

- People with ADHD may feel as though they are more special than other people because they are so different. This can lead them to internalizing this feeling of uniqueness as being better or smarter than others which can cause serious self-esteem issues even if many people think of them as "special" or "intellectual.

Women with ADHD may also have other learning disabilities.

When people are diagnosed with ADHD at a young age, they start out being taught coping strategies and self-management techniques in order to help them deal more effectively with the disorder. One of the easiest ways for these individuals to learn how cope with these issues is by using a list of things that they need to do or look at while they are engaged in some specific activity. It is very easy for someone who has ADHD to forget what they are supposed to be doing so often it helps if they have an aide reminding them what needs done. This list serves as a way for the person to stay focused on what they are doing. If one step of the process is done, then it helps them remember that they need to go to the next step or do something afterward.

How Is ADHD Treated?

A lot of people believe ADHD to be a completely fabricated disorder, but the truth is, many individuals do suffer from this condition, which can cause chronic issues with behavior and concentration. It is important that you know how ADHD is diagnosed and treated so that you are able to get the treatment that will work best for your loved one.

Though ADHD is a diagnosable condition, it's not something that you can't manage on your own. You don't have to learn how to power through your day with the best of them when you're in full control. With the right education and understanding, ADHD can be managed to some degree or made manageable. Therapy and treatment may not be necessary for every individual but it's nothing to turn away from without first considering if it could help you do what you need or want to do now. And therapy has many benefits that other treatments lack. It teaches coping skills, self-care habits, mindfulness techniques which all help people feel stronger and more capable in their daily lives.

One of the biggest things that therapy can teach you is how to tend to your mental health on a daily basis. Those who need therapy also typically need other treatments like coaching, medication, and self-help books. But therapy can be the base for all of these types of treatment. It teaches the skills for each other form of treatment that it takes for you to keep up with your own mental health.

Therapy can help you feel more at peace in the world around you. A therapist has years of education and experience with dealing with ADHD and its various forms and symptoms (of which there are many). Not only is it a place to relax and think more on things, it's also a place to get support that can help you deal with your symptoms on the inside.

Here are four ways therapy can help you:

1. Help You Feel at Peace with Yourself

Self-improvement in any form is hard. But treating your ADHD differently than it's treated by everyone else can feel like an impossible task. But when you have a therapist who can understand the problems of ADHD and knows how to handle them well, it becomes easier to manage all of those symptoms that may be bothering you.

There's no other treatment that can match the benefits of therapy, and for good reason. Therapy is the one treatment that teaches you how to think about your own thoughts and emotions in a different way. As a result, you will see your world differently and approach issues more calmly than before.

2. Help You Understand Others' ADHD Symptoms

It's easy to feel like you're all alone in this daily struggle when no one else can understand what you're going through. But with a therapist who has experience helping people who deal with

This is a big deal. When you get a diagnosis, it's tough to know how to act around others. If your symptoms are causing problems in your life, you may not be able to go out in public without feeling on edge or unsure of what's happening. But a therapist will introduce you to other people who also deal with ADHD and other mental health issues.

You will learn different ways of dealing with problems and how to pick up on small details that others miss that could make the difference between succeeding and failing at work or at school. This is training that you need but most people miss out on because they're too busy focusing on their own problems without realizing the potential for how helpful this benefit can be in their everyday lives.

3. Teach You Calm Techniques for Handling Stress and Boredom

 In fact, the symptoms can cause you to think about them more than necessary, which in turn fuels the problem and encourages it to grow.

It's natural for people with ADHD to feel stressed out or bored at times but that doesn't mean that it's necessary for you to allow these feelings take over your life every day. A therapist with experience in ADHD will know how to draw your attention to the things in life you often miss, like the captivating beauty of a passing flower or the new opportunity that awaits you at work.

4. Help You Learn How to Deal with Your Environment

A therapist will help introduce you to new techniques for managing your environment. If you're wondering why your daily life feels so unpredictable, it may be because of your inability to deal with change well.

Therapy teaches you how to calm down and think about yourself and the world around you objectively. It also teaches you how to think about your life holistically, instead of focusing on the small details that can get in the way of your happiness.

Therapy is going to help you feel more confident about your life as a whole. That's what most people need when they're dealing with ADHD symptoms–someone who understands what they're going through and can help them find a healthy way to relieve their stress.

If you still aren't sure if therapy is right for you, relax and don't be too hard on yourself for feeling this way. It's hard to know if you're ready for a change in your life. But therapy can help you see your problems from a different perspective and allow you to think about them in a way that promotes change, rather than discourages it.

Don't waste another second doubting yourself! If you feel like therapy sounds right for you, take the first step and make an appointment today!

Once you understand how it will help you deal with your ADHD from a new perspective, then it won't matter if any other part of your life isn't going the way that you want it to.

You'll Be Able to Find a Great Therapist

Finding the right therapist for ADHD can be a difficult process, especially if you've never considered it before.

The best way to find a great therapist is to look through their profiles and see if they have any reviews from other clients. Another great thing to do is ask your friends and relatives who have taken therapy elsewhere before.

Do they specialize in ADHD and other mental health disorders? Are they a licensed clinician? Will they work with both adults and adolescents? These are all important things that you'll need to know beforehand.

Setting Up an Appointment and What to Expect When You're There

The best way to get started with therapy is by contacting your insurance provider and finding out what kind of coverage your policy has. If you've been having trouble getting a diagnosis for ADHD, this is a great opportunity for you to finally get the help that you need.

Therapy And Cure for ADHD

Attention deficit hyperactivity disorder (ADHD) is a type of mental disorder characterized by problems with inattention, hyperactivity, and impulsiveness. ADHD affects an estimated 6-7% of women, making it the most commonly diagnosed childhood disorder. In recent years, scientists have made significant progress in understanding how the brain works and what factors contribute to

ADHD symptoms. However, because there are no drugs or medications that can cure or treat ADHD, therapists and parents often turn to alternative methods of treatment to manage its symptoms.

The therapy

Behavioral therapy is the most common form of therapy used to treat ADHD in women. It helps them to better control their behavior and eventually stay organized, focused and on-task. In behavioral therapy, women learn how to improve their self-management skills at home and at school. They also learn ways to deal with their impulses and how to make better decisions when faced with difficult situations. Research has shown that behavioral therapy is one of the most effective methods for treating ADHD in women.

The drugs

A stimulant drug like Ritalin or Adderall can improve symptoms of ADHD by increasing levels of the neurotransmitter's dopamine and norepinephrine in the brain. These medications work by increasing the release of these chemicals from nerve tissue. Many parents worry that a child will lose weight if they use these drugs to treat ADHD. In fact, some women who take stimulant medications may actually gain weight as they become more active and less sedentary. The stimulant drugs are not designed to cure ADHD; instead, they are used in combination with behavioral therapy to treat symptoms associated with the disorder.

The surgery

Cingulotomy is a surgical procedure that blocks areas of the brain's frontal lobes that regulate behavior and behavior control. This procedure is currently used to treat repetitive behavior, such as the compulsive behavior that some women with ADHD display. The surgery involves a surgeon inserting a burr into the frontal lobe. This technique enables the surgeon to limit activity in the area of the frontal lobes so that it can't cause unwanted behaviors. Other forms of neurostimulation have also been used in some parts of the world for treating ADHD, including deep brain stimulation and transcranial magnetic stimulation. These procedures involve placing electrodes or coils inside of certain regions of the brain to control certain symptoms associated with ADHD.

The alternative therapies

Many parents find that alternative therapy is more effective than behavioral therapy or drug treatment for controlling symptoms of ADHD in women. Alternative therapies include dietary changes, vitamins and supplements, homeopathy, Ayurveda and herbal medicine. Experts believe that several of these alternative treatments actually work by increasing the brain's neurotransmitters and inducing certain chemicals in the brain.

Synthetic diets

One popular alternative treatment for ADHD is a synthetic diet, which has been used in more than 50 countries around the world to treat women with ADHD. This diet restricts certain types of foods that commonly cause allergic reactions in people who suffer from ADHD. The theory is that reducing intake of these allergens will reduce or eliminate allergic reactions and other symptoms associated with ADHD. This diet requires parents to feed their women an extremely limited list of allowed foods (e.g. celery, zucchini, bananas, oatmeal and rice) for a few weeks or months. As the restrictions are gradually lifted, parents can slowly introduce more foods into their child's diet. A study conducted in Italy reports that nutritional supplements are effective in treating ADHD symptoms of women who have low levels of certain vitamin and mineral nutrients involved in normal brain function. These deficiencies impair neurotransmitter function and can cause symptoms of ADHD.

An Ayurvedic approach

Ayurvedic medicine is an alternative treatment designed to restore healthy states of mind and body. In India, it has been used for thousands of years to treat a wide variety of medical conditions including mild depression, anxiety disorders and attention deficit hyperactivity disorder (ADHD). Ayurvedic medicine uses herbs and natural products to promote detoxification of the body and mind.

The goal is to balance the autonomic nervous system, which controls automatic functions such as breathing, heart rate and digestion. The approach encourages healthy eating habits that include minimal gastric acidity and a diet free from excessively cold foods and spices.

Homeopathic remedies

Homeopaths believe that symptoms of ADHD can be treated by giving patients natural products that contain trace amounts of substances that cause ADHD in healthy people. Homeopathic remedies help to stimulate healthy neurophysiology by stimulating neurotransmitters in the brain.

Vitamin supplements

Supplementation with certain vitamins can be a useful treatment for ADHD in women who are deficient in specific nutrients. Deficiency of vitamin B6 and zinc, for example, has been linked to symptoms of inattention. Experts recommend using a multivitamin that contains vitamins B6 and zinc.

An herbal formula

Kappa is one type of Ayurvedic formula that can be used as a natural remedy for managing ADHD symptoms in women. It is believed to have a calming and sedative-like effect on the body. Kappa helps to balance the Vat osha, which controls movement and emotions. The formula is made up of eleven herbs including Brahmi (Canella Asiatic), Shankhapushpi (Convolvulus pluricaulis) and Vacha (Acorus clams). These herbs are believed to have anti-stimulant and calming effects that can help women with ADHD.

Kappa is best given to women who suffer from anxiety, restlessness and hyperactivity. It is also recommended for women whose ADHD symptoms are associated with physical excesses or suppressed emotions. These symptoms include having high blood pressure, a fast pulse rate or slow digestion.

A combination of homeopathic remedies and Ayurvedic herbal formulas has been successful in controlling the symptoms of ADHD in many women who don't respond well to behavioral therapy or drug treatment. A team of experts may be needed to help parents select the right alternative treatment for their child's ADHD symptoms and recommend the best regimen for them.

Conclusion

As of now, there is very little information on ADHD in women since only a few studies have been conducted on this population. Women have recently been diagnosed and treated with ADHD, and today, the majority of what one believes about this population is based on the scientific expertise of mental health specialists who have spent considerable time counseling women. ADHD in small children is often overlooked, the reasons for which remain unknown, and often females are not evaluated until they are adults. Occasionally, a woman becomes aware of her ADHD after one of her children receives a diagnosis. When she explores ADHD, she notices a plethora of parallel cases of herself. Few women seek care for ADHD because their lives are out of control; their finances may be in disarray; their administrative job and record-keeping are often ineffectively overseen; they may struggle futilely to stay aware of the demands of their positions; and they may feel much less prepared to stay aware of the day-by-day tasks of meals, food, and life overall. Different women are more successful because they are isolated from all their ADHD, fighting bravely to remain mindful of increasingly problematic demands by working late into the evening and investing their spare time trying to "get coordinated." If a woman's life is clearly in disarray or she can hide her struggles, she often presents herself as overwhelmed and exhausted.

Although research into ADHD in women lags behind that in men, more clinicians are finding important issues and co-occurring symptoms in women with ADHD. Women with ADHD may be prone to binge eating, alcohol abuse, and chronic sleep deprivation. Women with ADHD also feel dysphoria, severe sadness, and tension issues, as well as troublesome and anxiety symptoms like men with ADHD. Regardless, women with ADHD tend to have more emotional suffering and have poorer mental self-esteem than men with ADHD. Women diagnosed with ADHD in adulthood are more likely to have burdensome side effects, to be more pushed and restless, to have a more external locus of control, to have poorer morale, and to be more locked in adopting practices that are feeling-oriented than task-situated. According to studies, having a parent with ADHD puts a strain on the whole family. However, women may experience more anxiety than men because they are more responsible for their homes and children. Furthermore, ongoing research suggests that husbands of women with ADHD are less tolerant of their partner's ADHD than spouses of men with ADHD. Persistent pressure harms women with ADHD, affecting their mental health. Women that experience chronic stress, such as that associated with ADHD, are more vulnerable to illnesses associated with chronic stress, such as fibromyalgia. As a result, it is becoming increasingly clear that the lack of proper diagnosis and treatment of ADHD in women is a critical public health problem.

If you have made it this far, a situation or two must have appealed to you. You most probably have so much in common with the practical examples brought to light. ADHD has been defined, and the different types have been outlined to facilitate the process for potentially undiagnosed or misdiagnosed women with ADHD. There is no denying that women with ADHD are misunderstood and overlooked in society. The idea is not to take the spotlight away from men and young boys with ADHD but rather shed light on women and their ADHD.

Addressing the main concerns for women with ADHD means no stone is left unturned. Understanding cues, the body gives off can help women keep an eye out for potential ADHD symptoms. Getting the right diagnoses can often mean scouting around for the best medical advice and seeking a practitioner you feel comfortable with, who also happens to have the right experience and sources to diagnose you. Women with ADHD require assistance and support throughout their lives. Some may have the luxury of having a great support system, making things easier for them. Others may need to be more perseverant to manage their lives and those of their children independently. Women with ADHD need to learn that all their failed tries and mistakes have shaped them and made them who they are. It does not stop at that. There are plenty of skills one can have and sources one can go to cues, help manage their finances, daily schedules, emotions, and relationships.

Learn to use your best skills and overcome the weaker ones. Do not let your ADHD define you because you are more than your ADHD. Begin to enjoy yourself. To begin with, you have no power over your genetics. ADHD is a psychological condition, and self-control alone would not be enough to overcome genetics. Creativity, intuition, and resilience are also hereditary traits that are often associated with ADHD. Knowing all about this disorder can help everyone cope with it better. Help yourself understand that you need relief and assistance. This need fuels your creativity and allows you to excel in high-risk or high-stress situations. Choose activities where your ADHD characteristics can support rather than hinder you, helping you feel accomplished and fulfilled. Know that you are unique and always remember ADHD doesn't make you less human; your brain just doesn't stick to the "acceptable" way of living set by society. Don't make ADHD an excuse but rather the fuel that empowers you to get all your heart desires. I believe in you!! Believe in yourself and GO GET IT!!!